Medieval Latin
A Beginner's Self-Study Guide

The 2nd Edition

Luke Daly

FOREWORD

Learning Latin is crucial for historians studying charters, wills, and testaments because Latin was the dominant language of legal, administrative, and ecclesiastical documents in medieval Europe. Understanding Latin allows historians to access these primary sources in their original form, providing direct insight into the legal practices, social structures, and cultural norms of the time.

Charters, for instance, are legal documents that record the transfer of property, the granting of rights, or the establishment of privileges. They offer a wealth of information about land ownership, social hierarchies, and the relationship between lords and vassals. By studying these documents, historians can trace the development of feudal systems, the rise of towns, and the economic foundations of medieval society.

Wills and testaments are equally revealing. They often include detailed inventories of personal property, information about family relations, and the social obligations of the deceased. Through these documents, historians can gain insight into the material culture of the past, the distribution of wealth, and the ways in which individuals sought to secure their legacy.

Moreover, the language and terminology used in these documents can reveal shifts in legal and social concepts over time. Latin's precise and formal nature helped to standardise legal practices across different regions, making it an essential tool for historians who wish to understand the broader legal and cultural landscape of medieval Europe.

In sum, Latin provides historians with the linguistic key to unlock the rich details contained in charters, wills, and testaments, offering a clearer understanding of the past's legal, social, and economic dynamics.

The aim of this book, therefore, is to enable anyone with little or no prior experience of the language to tackle the Latin they are likely to encounter in Medieval or Early Modern documents such as charters or wills. The joy of using this self-taught guide is that it allows you to learn at your own pace and revisit topics you may have found challenging.

Moreover, the guide aims to introduce the reader to forms of Latin documents that are likely to be useful in higher and further education, such as wills, manorial records, and deeds, with a focus on standard formulae and specialised vocabulary.

This book concentrates on Latin-to-English translation. Whilst the reader may find it useful to memorise some of the basic grammatical forms, the grammar sheets and word list at the back of this book are designed to assist the reader in translation as much as possible. Written exercises or short translations are also provided throughout this book to enable the reader to put into practice what they have learnt.

As such, this guide serves as an introduction to translating administrative materials within Anglo-Latin sphere of the Late Medieval Era.

This is best used as supplementary material alongside other works such as:

- *Dictionary of Medieval Latin from British Sources*
- *C.R. Cheney's Handbook of Dates: For Students of British History*
- *Eileen A. Gooder's Latin for Local History: An Introcution*
- *Adriano Cappelli's Dizionario di Abbreviature*
- *The Oxford Handbook of Latin Palaeography*

As of 2024, a revised second edition has been created in response to the feedback and reviews received over the past years since the book's original release. These revisions mainly address grammatical errors and improvements to readability.

About the Author

Luke Daly is a highly accomplished Medieval Historian, known for his in-depth research and engaging storytelling. Holding a bachelor's and distinction master's degree in medieval history from the University of East Anglia, he is embarking on groundbreaking research into the financial records of Canterbury Cathedral, aiming to shed light on Christian monasticism within England from 1200 to 1300.

In addition to his academic pursuits, Luke is a prolific author. He self-published his first book, Medieval Latin: A Beginner's Self-Taught Guide, in November 2021 through Amazon Kindle Direct Publishing. This comprehensive guide has seen great success, with copies sold internationally. Moreover, he recently published "*Medieval Saints and Their Sins: A New History of the Middle Ages Through Saints and Their Stories*" with Pen and Sword Publishing.

Yet, Luke's passion for history extends beyond the written word. He hosts a popular podcast, "The Daly Medieval Podcast," which has gained a devoted following on platforms such as YouTube and Spotify. Through the podcast, Luke not only shares captivating historical narratives but also conducts interviews with professionals, authors, and fellow historians, enriching the listeners' understanding of the past.

Contents

Chapter	Page

Section II: Miscellaneous Items

Latin Compared to English

Medieval Latin is not a particularly difficult language as it has a limited vocabulary and a methodical set of rules that allow you to decode even the most complex of sentences.

Believe it or not, the best way to learn Latin is to begin by analysing and understanding English grammar. The reason for this will become clearer as we venture on, but to begin with let us look at the following sentence:

The girl sees a dog.

Ask yourself this:

- *What is the indefinite article in this sentence?*
- *What is the definite article?*
- *What is the subject?*
- *What is the object?*
- *What are the nouns?*

When I first learnt Latin as 20-year-old university student, I was posed with a similar sentence and these questions. It astounded me, however, that although English is my mother-tongue, I had difficulty breaking down the sentence into its grammatical forms – *What even is an indefinite article?*

The key to translating Latin is found in these grammatical questions as by understanding nouns, articles, and declensions, you will be able to translate medieval charters, manuscripts, and wills with ease.

The girl sees a dog.

'The' and 'A' are both known as **articles**. More specifically, 'A' is an **indefinite article** as it refers to something non-specific, such as a dog. 'The', on the other hand, is a **definite article** as it refers to something specific, in this case, the girl.

In Medieval Latin, there are no articles, nor are there words that translate directly to 'A' or 'The'. This can make translation challenging, as you must insert these articles yourself

Now, let us examine the subject and object of the sentence above.

The subject refers to the word that the sentence is about—'Who' is performing the action in the sentence. In this example, it is the girl who is seeing a dog, so 'the girl' is the subject.

The object of the sentence refers to the word or thing that receives the action from the subject. In this example, since the girl is seeing a dog, the dog is therefore the object of the sentence.

This is important to understand as in Latin, the ending of a word tells you whether it is the subject, or object.

To show this, here is the same sentence but in Medieval Latin:

Puella videt Canem

Puella – Girl

Videt – He/She/It Sees

Canem – Dog

Translating this sentence directly means "Girl sees dog" which is why you then must input the articles '*A*' and '*The*' yourself.

The '-a' ending of *Puella* tells us that it is the **subject**, and the '-em' ending of *Canem* shows us that this is the **object**.

If we switch the sentence to "The dog sees a girl" whereby the dog is now the subject and the girl is the object you will see the endings change in Latin:

Canis videt Puellam

Taking note of the word endings is crucial as there is **no word order in Latin** unlike in English. This means that whilst the sentence "*The girl sees a dog*" can only be written one way in English, in Latin it could be written as:

Puella videt Canem.

Canem Puella videt.

Videt Puella Canem.

The key is the **noun endings**, which in Latin are called *Cases*.

Noun Cases

In Medieval Latin, there are 6 noun cases – but for the purposes of charters, there are 5 main ones. These are as follows:

- *NOMINATIVE – The subject of a sentence*
- *ACCUSATIVE – The object of a sentence*
- *GENITIVE – A possessive noun / 'Of'*
- *DATIVE – 'To' or 'For'*
- *ABLATIVE – 'By', 'With' or 'From'*

The sixth case is commonly found in the Bible and is referred to as the *Vocative*. This case refers to a declaration or address of someone such as saying "O Lord..." It is commonly missed out as it is rarely found in wills and charters.

Nevertheless, the easiest way to understand these cases is to, once again, analyse them using English. We have already looked at subject and object nouns in sentences and so let us move on to the three other cases.

Genitive

The Genitive case is used for prepositions:

"I am using Anne's Pencil"

English has adopted the use of the apostrophe for prepositions as seen in the example, but for the purposes of Medieval Latin, we would translate "Anne's Pencil" as "the pencil of Anne".

The use of *'of'* in this example is the Genitive case.

Dative

The Dative case in Latin tells us the indirect object of a verb. In other words, whether the object receiver is the recipient or beneficiary of an action.

A recipient is expressed by the word *"for"*, and a beneficiary is expressed by the word *"to"*.

A sentence example could be:

- "Anne buys a pencil for Roger"
- "Anne gives a pencil to Roger"

When translating from Latin to English you will have to decide whether the sentence needs either 'to' or 'for' if the noun is dative.

Ablative

The final case is Ablative. Quite simply this case is used to express 'By', 'With' or 'From'. For example:

- "I bought this land from the Lord"
- "Anne bought fruit with Peter"
- "Roger lives by the church"

It is rare, however, to have a sentence with just one case. Take for instance this sentence:

Robertus filius Willelmi dat terram suam domino.

This translates to:

"Robert, the son of William, gives his land to the Lord."

This sentence contains a nominative, an accusative, a genitive, and a dative noun. But what noun correlates to which case?

Nominative – Robert

Accusative – Land

Genitive – Of William

Dative – To the Lord

It is important to grasp this concept of noun cases as otherwise it may trip you up – but just remember to look at the endings!

Note: Words of the same ending will almost always follow the same case.

"Robertus Filius Willelmi"

How do you know that Robertus Filius Willelmi is 'Robert, son of William', and not 'William, son of Robert'?

Robertus Filius **both end in '-us'** whilst *Willelmi* ends in '-i'. This means that *Robertus* and *Filius* are both nominative and follow the same case, whilst Willelmi is dative.

Noun Case Endings – Terra, Dominus, Pratum

As covered, nouns can be governed by 5 cases. But each case has its own set of endings. This chapter will cover the most common 1st and 2nd Declension nouns and their endings.

First Declension Nouns:

First Declension nouns are almost always feminine and quite possibly are the most common set of nouns found in Latin. For the purposes of this guide, we will be looking at 'Terra' meaning 'Land' as this is extremely common in charters.

CASE	Singular	Plural	
Nominative	Terra	Terre	*Subject*
Accusative	Terram	Terras	*Object*
Genitive	Terre	Terrarum	*Of*
Dative	Terre	Terris	*To/For*
Ablative	Terra	Terris	*By/With/From*

You may notice that some of these noun forms have the same endings. Quite simply it is up to you to decide which case the noun is referring to in a sentence – however, it should be clear which it is by the context of the sentence.

Second Declension

Second Declension Nouns have two genders: masculine and neuter. Like First Declension nouns, these noun endings are very popular. For this guide, we will be using the masculine noun *'Dominus'* meaning *'Lord'* and the neuter noun *'Pratum'* meaning *'Meadow'*.

Masc. "Dominus":

CASE	Singular	Plural	
Nominative	Dominus	Domini	*Subject*
Accusative	Dominum	Dominos	*Object*
Genitive	Domini	Dominorum	*Of*
Dative	Domino	Dominis	*To/For*
Ablative	Domino	Dominis	*By/With/From*

An issue many Latin students come across is how to translate *'Domine'*. *Domine* is the genitive (or dative) form of the First Declension noun *Domina,* which means, *'**The Lady**'*.

None of the case endings of *Domina* and *Dominus* overlap and so it should be easy to separate them.

Neuter. "Pratum":

CASE	Singular	Plural	
Nominative	Pratum	Prata	*Subject*
Accusative	Pratum	Prata	*Object*
Genitive	Prati	Patorum	*Of*
Dative	Prato	Pratis	*To/For*
Ablative	Prato	Pratis	*By/With/From*

Let's examine some Latin sentences using everything we have covered thus far. For the purposes of focusing on nouns, all you need to understand with verbs is the following:

(Singular)   **vowel + t — He/She/It**

(Plural)   **vowel + nt — They**

Some of the most popular verbs are:

- Dat— He/She/It Gives
- Dant — *They Give*

- Tenet — *He/She/It Holds*
- Tenent— They Hold

When translating the following sentences, be sure to look at the endings and refer to the tables above.

Translate:

1. Tenet messuagium
2. Dant domum
3. Tenent acram

Answers:

1. *He holds a messuage*
2. *They give a house*
3. *They hold an acre*

Note that an **adjective describing a noun has the same case, gender, and number as the noun** they accompany.

- Un<u>am</u> acr<u>am</u> – one acre
- Un<u>um</u> denari<u>um</u> – one penny
- Su<u>o</u> Domin<u>o</u> – to/from his lord

Here are some sentences that include **singular dative and ablative** endings. These end in **-o**:

1. Dat suum messuagium Philippo

2. Tenent suam acram domino

3. Reddit unum denarium Willelmo

Answers:

1. *He gives his messuage to Philip*

2. *They hold their acre from the Lord*

3. *He pays one penny to William*

Further, here are some more which contain either dative or ablative **plural** endings. These end in **-is**:

4. Philippus dat unam acram filiis suis.

5. Willelmus tenet terram serviciis debitis.

6. Predictus Robertus reddit unum denarium dominis.

Answers:

4. *Philip gives one acre to his sons*

5. *William holds land by services owed* (feudal obligation)

6. *The aforsaid Robert pays one penny to the Lords*

Often charters will avoid confusion of cases by using nouns following the prepositions *cum* (with), *de* (of), and *pro* (for, in return for). These nouns will be in the **ablative**.

1. Willelmus domum cum uno gardino tenet
2. Philippus reddit domino unum denarium pro suo messuagio

Answers:

1. *William holds a house with one garden*
2. *Philip pays to the lord one penny for his messuage*

Currently, we have been using the verbs *Tenet* and *Dat*. The following, however, are more common verbs you will come across in Medieval Latin:

- Reddit – He/She/It Pays
- Reddunt – They Pay

- Concedit – He/She/It Grants
- Concedunt – They Grant

- Debet – He/She/It Owes
- Debent – They Owe

Using the new vocabulary, you will be able to translate the following advanced sentences which use the **accusative plural**. These end in **-os** and **-as** and are the object of a verb:

1. Philippus concedit suas terras

2. Concedunt duos gardinos domino

3. Robertus Willelmo tres acras dat

Answers:

1. *Philip grants his lands*

2. *They grant two gardens to the lord*

3. *Robert gives three acres to William*

Let us finish this chapter by doing the same for the **genitive plural**. These will end in **-arum** and **-orum**:

1. Willelmus reddit summam duorum denariorum

2. Robertus debet redditum duarum librarum

Answers:

1. *William pays the sum of two pennies*

2. *Robert owes a rent of two pounds*

Hic, Hec, Hoc

The last couple of chapters form the basic foundations of the Latin language. I would strongly recommend that you are able to grasp **noun cases** before you move on as from hereafter, each chapter will be building upon this basis.

This chapter aims to introduce *Hic*, meaning *This or These.*

When an adjective is associated with a noun, they must agree in the following ways:

1. **Number** – Singular or Plural
2. **Gender** – Masculine, Feminine, or Neuter
3. **Case** – Nominative, Accusative, Genitive, etc.

With that in mind, let us introduce the adjective '*Hic*' and its declension.

Hic – This

	Singular		
CASE	**Masculine**	**Feminine**	**Neuter**
Nominative	Hic	Hec	Hoc
Accusative	Hunc	Hanc	Hoc
Genitive	Huius	Huius	Huius
Dative	Huic	Huic	Huic
Ablative	Hoc	Hac	Hoc

	Plural		
CASE	**Masculine**	**Feminine**	**Neuter**
Nominative	Hi	He	Hec
Accusative	Hos	Has	Hec
Genitive	Horum	Harum	Horum
Dative	Hiis	Hiis	Hiis
Ablative	Hiis	Hiis	Hiis

The reason why we establish that adjectives follow nouns is that *Hec*, for example, could be:

- Singular, Feminine, Nominative
- Plural, Neuter, Nominative
- Plural, Neuter, Accusative

To know which to use, simply look at the noun it is associated with. Let us look at some examples:

Episcopus est dominus **huius** feodi

*The bishop is the lord of **this** fee*

As *feodi* is **Singular, Neuter, and Genitive**, then using the chart above we would use the form *Huius.*

Translate the following sentences which contain a form of *hic, hec, hoc*:

1. Robertus reddit **hos** tres denarios pro **hoc** messuagio

2. Hic filius Roberti tenet **hanc** terram pro **hiis** serviciis

3. Galfridus tenet **hoc** feodum de episcopo de Norwico

Answers:

1. *Robert pays these three pennies for this messuage*

2. *This son of Robert holds this land for these services*

3. *Geoffry holds this fee of the bishop of Norwich*

Dates and times are given in the ablative.

Hoc anno Willelmus et Robertus tenent has duas acras de domina

This year, William and Robert hold these two acres from the Lady

Hic, Hec, Hoc may also be used as a pronoun on its own:

1. Thomas tenet hanc domum; Thomas tenet hanc.

2. Episcopus reddit tres libras; episcopus reddit has

1. Thomas holds this house; Thomas holds it.

3. The bishop pays three pounds; the bishop pays it.

21

"... et hac carta confirmat"

In medieval charters, when a transaction is made (usually property, land, or money) to someone, it is legally bound and 'confirmed' by a charter.

It is these charters that we are aiming to be able to translate by the end of this book.

As such, the phrase *'et hac carta confirmat'* (the forms may differ depending on the subject) is deployed which means *'and confirm by this charter'*.

Here is an example of its use:

Henricus filius predicti domini Roberti terras predictas dat **et hac carta confirmat** ecclesie Sancti Johannis Baptiste.

This translates to:

Henry, the son of the aforesaid Lord Robert, gives and **confirms by this charter** *the aforesaid lands to the church of St. John the Baptist.*

Another version of this phrase is:

... et hoc scripto confirmavit.

This means **'and confirmed by this writing'** and is simply just another expression that a transaction is legally confirmed.

First and Second Declension Adjectives -

Predictus

Echoing a point made in the previous chapter. Adjectives must agree with the noun they describe in:

1. **Number** – Singular or Plural
2. **Gender** – Masculine, Feminine, or Neuter
3. **Case** – Nominative, Accusative, Genitive, etc.

Adjectives have declensions just like nouns, and this chapter follows the First and Second Declension.

An extremely common adjective used in Medieval Latin is *'Predictus'* which means *'the aforesaid'*.

If the associated noun is a **Second Declension noun and Masculine**, then Predictus will also follow the Second Declension endings:

(Nom.) *Predictus Dominus – The aforesaid lord*

(Acc.) *Predictum Dominum*

(Gen.) *Pridicti Domini*

(Dat.) *Predicto Domino*

(Abl.) *Predicto Domino*

If, however, the associated noun is **feminine and 1st Declension**, *Predictus* will follow First Declension endings.

(Nom.) *Predicta Via – The aforesaid road*

(Acc.) *Predictam Viam*

(Gen.) *Pridicte Vie*

(Dat.) *Predicte Vie*

(Abl.) *Predicta Via*

You may notice that for First and Second Declension declension nouns, the adjective **merely copies the same ending**. This is a nice shortcut to see which noun the adjective is describing and are often referred to as **us, a, um adjectives** (each corresponding to masculine, feminine, and neuter nominative singular endings).

Adjectives in dictionaries will often be given in this form.

Bonus, -a, -um – Good

Whilst this does work for First and Second declension nouns, it falls short on Third declension nouns as these are irregular.

As an exercise to grasp case endings, with the following sentences, give the correct form of *Predictus* for each noun:

1. Robertus concedit terras.
2. Robertus dat tres acras Domino.

Answers:

1. ***Predictus*** *Robertus concedit* ***predictas*** *terras.*

2. ***Predictus*** *Robertus dat **predictas** tres acras **predicto** domino.*

In terms of charters, *Predictus* is by far the most common, but there are other words frequently found in Medieval Latin charters that translate and follow nouns in the same way, namely:

- *Supradictus*
- *Supernominatus*
- *Suprascruptus*

The first two translate as 'the above-mentioned', and *Suprascriptus* which translates as 'the above-written'.

Translate the following:

Ricardus filius predicti Willelmi terras predictas dat et hac carta confirmat ecclesie Sancti Nicholai.

Answer:

Richard, the son of the aforesaid William gives and confirms by this charter the aforesaid land to the church of St. Nicholas.

Present and Perfect Verbs

Already we have introduced some common verbs but more attention should be given to them to properly understand their forms.

All verbs come under **4 groups**, and each group has a set of different endings for each pronoun. Here is a table of **present verbs** and their endings.

For the purposes of ease, the examples below are:

- *Group 1: Confirmo – I Confirm*
- *Group 2: Teneo – I Hold*
- *Group 3: Concedo – I Grant*
- *Group 4: Servio – I Serve*

Present	Group 1	Group 2
I	Confirm–**o**	Ten–**eo**
You (s)	Confirm–**as**	Ten–**es**
He/She/It	Confirm–**at**	Ten–**et**
We	Confirm–**amus**	Ten–**emus**
You (pl)	Confirm–**atis**	Ten–**etis**
They	Confirm–**ant**	Ten–**ent**

Present	Group 3	Group 4
I	Conced–**o**	Serv–**io**
You (s)	Conced–**is**	Serv–**is**
He/She/It	Conced–**it**	Serv–**it**
We	Conced–**imus**	Serv–**imus**
You (pl)	Conced–**itis**	Serv–**itis**
They	Conced–**unt**	Serv–**iunt**

In a dictionary, such as the one at the back of this guide, often the verb will be given in its 'I' form with a number which correspondes to which group it falls within.

e.g.   *Clamo (1)* – To Claim

The **perfect tense** is a form of the **past tense** (in Medieval Latin there are a few different past tenses; perfect, imperfect, pluperfect) and it translates as such:

- *Group 1: Confirmavi – I Confirmed*
- *Group 2: Tenui – I Held*
- *Group 3: Concessi – I Granted*
- *Group 4: Servio – I Served*

Here is a table of the perfect tense with their new stems and endings:

Perfect	Group 1	Group 2
I	Confirmav–**i**	Tenu–**i**
You (s)	Confirmav–**isti**	Tenu–**isti**
He/She/It	Confirmav–**it**	Tenu–**it**
We	Confirmav–**imus**	Tenu–**imus**
You (pl)	Confirmav–**istis**	Tenu–**istis**
They	Confirmav–**erunt**	Tenu–**erunt**

Perfect	Group 3	Group 4
I	Concess–**i**	Serviv–**i**
You (s)	Concess–**isti**	Serviv–**isti**
He/She/It	Concess–**it**	Serviv–**it**
We	Concess–**imus**	Serviv–**imus**
You (pl)	Concess–**istis**	Serviv–**istis**
They	Concess–**erunt**	Serviv–**erunt**

When comparing present and perfect verbs, you will notice that the stem changes within each group.

For Group 1 verbs, the present stem: **Confirm-** changes to the perfect stem: **Confirmav-**

In other words, the stem of Group 1 verbs gain '**av**' when in the perfect tense. The other groups also extend their stems:

In Group 2, the present stem: **Ten-** changes to become the perfect stem **Tenu-,** thus gaining '**u**'.

Group 3 verbs are **irregular** meaning that **the whole stem changes** in the perfect tense. Whilst the stem in the present tense is: **Conced-**, in the perfect tense it becomes **Concess-**

Note that dictionaries will give the present stem of Group 3 verbs followed by the infinitive, the perfect, and the supine:

e.g.   *Concedo, -ere, -cessi, -cessum* (3) – *To Confirm*

In Group 4, the present stem: **Serv-** changes to become the perfect stem **Serviv-,** thus gaining '**iv**'.

The saving grace of the perfect tense is that the verb endings are the same across all four groups. All that changes between words is the stem.

Translate:

1. Hec est finalis concordia facta in curia regis

2. Hac carta indentata virgatam terre Ranulpho confirmavimus

3. Has predictas sex acras terre Nicholaus concessit et hac carta confirmavit ecclesie Sancte Marie.

4. Anna filia predicti Roberti terram predictam concedit et hac carta confirmat monasterio Sancti Trinitatis.

Answers:

1. *This is the final agreement made in the court of the King.*

2. *By this indented charter we confirmed the yard of land of Ranulph*

3. *Nicholas granted and confirmed by this charter the aforesaid six acres of land to the church of St. Mary*

4. *Anna, the daughter of the aforesaid Robert, grants and confirms by this charter the aforesaid land to the monastery of the Holy Trinity.*

If you completed these questions with success and have grasped the concepts of each chapter thus far, then have successfully understood the foundations of Medieval Latin.

If, however, you did struggle on some of the concepts, all you need to do is revisit earlier chapters until you are more comfortable. The joy of this book is that your Latin journey is defined by you.

Nevertheless, no matter how large or difficult a charter or will may get, it all builds upon these founding blocks. The remaining content is about adding onto this foundation with more noun declensions, verb tenses, pronouns, numbers, dates, and charter terminology.

Whilst at the moment you can tackle a couple of Latin lines, by the end of this book, you will be able to translate large paragraphs from medieval charters and be able to take on the archives!

Personal Pronouns

In typical Latin fashion, the best way to understand Latin pronouns is to first analyse the English language. In English we have three main 'Persons' that contain pronouns:

- 1st Person: I, My, We
- 2nd Person: You
- 3rd Person: He, She, It, They, Their, His, Hers

All of these words have Latin counterparts and different endings in accordance to each case. To begin with let us look at personal pronouns:

	I	You (s)	He/She/It/ They	We	You (pl)
Nom.	Ego	Tu		Nos	Vos
Acc.	Me	Te	Se	Nos	Vos
Gen.	Mei	Tui	Sui	Nostri/ Nostrum	Vesti/ Vestrum
Dat.	Mihi	Tibi	Sibi	Nobis	Vobis
Abl.	Me	Te	Se	Nobis	Vobis

Most of the time you will only be using personal pronouns in the **nominative** – namely *'Ego'* and *'Nos'* at the beginning of a charter.

As our questions get increasingly more challenging, the use of *my, his, hers, and their,* is more frequently deployed. For example saying "**My** brother and **his** son give **their** land to the Lord…"

These words are expressed by **Meus, Suus, and Eius**. Its declension is the same as other First and Second Declension adjectives:

Meus – My

Singular	Masc.	Fem.	Neuter
Nom.	Meus	Mea	Meum
Acc.	Meum	Meam	Meum
Gen.	Mei	Mee	Mei
Dat.	Meo	Mee	Meo
Abl.	Meo	Mea	Meo

Suus – His/Her/Their

Singular	Masc.	Fem.	Neuter
Nom.	Suus	Sua	Suum
Acc.	Suum	Suam	Suum
Gen.	Sui	Sue	Sui
Dat.	Suo	Sue	Suo
Abl.	Suo	Sua	Suo

Euis – He/She/It/They/Her/His/Their

Singular	Masc.	Fem.	Neuter
Nom.	Is	Ea	Id
Acc.	Eum	Eam	Id
Gen.	Euis	Euis	Euis
Dat.	Ei	Ei	Ei
Abl.	Eo	Ea	Eo

Qui, Que, Quod

In the previous chapter we had a look at the different types of pronouns and their corresponding Latin versions. This, however, is not the end of it as pronouns in a sentence can replace a noun to avoid repetition. Take for instance this following sentence:

"James saw Lucy. Lucy looked at James and smiled."

The repetition of 'Lucy' and 'James' can be replaced using pronouns:

"James saw Lucy. **She** looked at **him** and smiled."

Pronouns also allows us to combine **clauses**.

There are two types of sentence clauses:

- Primary
- Subordinate

A primary clause is an independent sentence that makes sense on its own, for example, *"James saw Lucy."*

A subordinate clause is the dependent sentence that only makes sense in context with the primary sentence, for example, *"She looked at him and smiled."*

In English, we have specific pronouns that can be used to combine these clauses: **Who/Whom**

Here are some examples of English sentences deploying these pronouns:

"He passed me a pen, **which** I later lost."

"The man, **whom** I had seen last week, was here today."

"I thanked the waitress **who** had served me."

"We listened to the teacher, **by whose** instruction we followed."

"The family, **to whom** I babysat for, have now moved away."

You get the jist of it, but interestingly '*Who and Whom*' are one of the few words in English that have versions for each Latin case:

- Nominative – Who
- Accusative – Whom
- Genitive – Whose
- Dative – To Whom
- Ablative – With Which

To know which case the pronoun should be, you have to know which noun it is replacing.

"He passed me a pen, **which** I later lost."

The pen in this scenario is the object of the sentence and thus is <u>accusative</u>.

"I thanked the waitress **who** had served me."

In this scenario, however, as the waitress is the subject of the sentence, the pronoun is <u>nominative</u>.

The Latin version of Who/Whom is **Qui, Que, Quod**

The following table shows its declension:

Singular	Masculine	Feminine	Neuter
Nominative	Qui	Que	Quod
Accusative	Quem	Quam	Quod
Genitive	Cuius	Cuius	Cuius
Dative	Cui	Cui	Cui
Ablative	Quo	Qua	Quo

Plural	Masculine	Feminine	Neuter
Nominative	Qui	Que	Que
Accusative	Quos	Quas	Que
Genitive	Quorum	Quarum	Quorum
Dative			
Ablative		Quibus	

It is worth noting that when translating, if the noun that *qui, que, quod* is replacing is **inanimate**, such as land, then you would translate it as *which* rather than *who/whom*.

Let us look at some Latin examples:

    1. Henricus tenet messuagia, que iacent iuxta vie.

This translates as "*Henry holds messuages, which lie next to the road.*" Notice here that the form *que* is **Plural**

and Neuter to follow *messuagia* but is in the **Nominative form**.

You may question – how can this be nominative if *messuagia* is in the accusative case? Simply put, *qui, que, quod* follows the gender and number of the noun it replaces but **its case is determined by its position within the subordinate clause** (The messuages lie next to the road).

It may be a little confusing but as you are translating from Latin to English, whether the case is accusative, or nominative **won't matter too much** as both translate as which/who/whom.

Let us look at another examples:

2. Hec est Domina, **de qua** teneo meam terram.

*This is the lady, **from whom** I hold my land.*

Qua in this case is **singular and feminine** to follow *Domina*. This reason for the ablative form is because the subordinate clause could have been written as "I hold my land **from the lady**" and therefore as it is ablative, we use *Qua*.

Translate the following:

1. Hec est via, que ducit ad Norwicum

2. Robertus tenet messuagium, quod abbuttat super magnam ripam.

3. Lego uxori mee domum, in qua Iohannes filius meus manet.

36

4. Hic est dominus, de quo teneo meam terram.

5. He sunt filie, quibus do hoc pratum.

Answers:

1. *This is the road which leads to Norwich*

2. *Robert gives a messuage, which borders on the great bank*

3. *I bequeath to my wife the house, in which my son, John, remains.*

4. *This is the Lord, of which I hold my land.*

5. *These are the daughters, to whom I give this meadow.*

Here is a longer passage for you to translate:

Dominus Iohannes de Lond' dedit ecclesie Sancti Laurentii decem acras terre cum pertinenciis quas tenuit in Witchurch, quarum tres acras iacent inter terram Bernardi de Oxon' et terram Walteri Brewer.

Answer:

The Lord John of London gave to the church of St. Lawrence ten acres of land with its appurtenances which he held in Witchchurch, three acres of which lie between the land of Bernard of Oxford and the land of Walter Brewer.

Third and Fourth Declension Nouns

Thus far we have delt predominantly with First and Second Declension nouns. It is fair to say that within Medieval Latin, the majority of nouns can be attributed to either of these two declensions.

There are, however, some nouns that fall within the Third and Fourth Declension and though uncommon, we have already encountered some of these words before, such as *Domus* which is a Fourth Declension noun.

Let us firstly begin by understanding the forms of the Third Declension:

Singular	Masc. / Fem.	Neuter
Nominative	*Various*	*Various*
Accusative	*-em*	*Follow Nom.*
Genitive	*-is*	*-is*
Dative	*-i*	*-i*
Ablative	*-e*	*-e*

As you can see, it is a little more complicated than the straightforward endings the of previous declensions. To explain further, here is the singular form of the masculine Third Declension noun *'Miles'* meaning *'Knight'*:

- Nominative – Miles
- Accusative – Militem
- Genitive – Militis
- Dative – Militi
- Ablative – Milite

You may notice that the nominative stem is different from the others. **All Third Declension nouns will have a stem change.**

Here is the following noun endings for the Third Declension plural:

Plural	Masc. / Fem.	Neuter
Nominative	*-es*	*-a*
Accusative	*-es*	*-a*
Genitive	*-um*	*-um*
Dative	*-ibus*	*-ibus*
Ablative	*-ibus*	*-ibus*

Using '*Miles*' once again, here are the set of endings in the plural form:

- Nominative – Milites
- Accusative – Milites
- Genitive – Militum
- Dative – Militibus
- Ablative – Militibus

In the plural, **the nominative follows the changed stem** (in this case is *Milit-*).

Unfortunately, there is no formula of knowing the stem change of any Third Declension noun. However, Latin dictionaries should give you the **nominative and genitive form** of a said word which will tell you the stem change.

E.g.: *Miles, Militis* - Knight

The following are some common **Third Declension** nouns you probably will encounter:

Rex, Regis – King

Masculine	Singular	Plural
Nominative	*Rex*	*Reges*
Accusative	*Regem*	*Reges*
Genitive	*Regis*	*Regum*
Dative	*Regi*	*Regibus*
Ablative	*Rege*	*Regibus*

Nomen, Nominis – Name

Neuter	Singular	Plural
Nominative	*Nomen*	*Nomina*
Accusative	*Nomen*	*Nomina*
Genitive	Nominis	*Nominum*
Dative	*Nomini*	*Nominibus*
Ablative	*Nomine*	*Nominibus*

Pater, Patris - Father

Masculine	Singular	Plural
Nominative	*Pater*	*Patres*
Accusative	*Patrem*	*Patres*
Genitive	*Patris*	*Patrum*
Dative	*Patri*	*Patribus*
Ablative	*Patre*	*Patribus*

Mater, Matris – Mother

Feminine	Singular	Plural
Nominative	*Mater*	*Matres*
Accusative	*Matrem*	*Matres*
Genitive	*Matris*	*Matrum*
Dative	*Matri*	*Matribus*
Ablative	*Matre*	*Matribus*

The key aspect of the Third Declension is that the stem changes. However, let's move on to the **Fourth Declension.**

Like the Third Declension, it can be both masculine and feminine, but Fourth Declension neuters are extremely rare in medieval documents and so for ease we can avoid them.

This is an incredibly simple declension as you will see:

	Singular	Plural
Nominative	*-us*	*-us*
Accusative	*-um*	*-us*
Genitive	*-us*	*-uum*
Dative	*-ui*	*-ibus*
Ablative	*-u*	*-ibus*

Both masculine and feminine nouns have the same endings and can be easily recognised by the *-u* ending. To add to the ease, there is also no stem change.

41

Here is an example of the Fourth Declension using *'Obitus'* meaning *'Death'*:

Masculine	Singular	Plural
Nominative	*Obitus*	*Obitus*
Accusative	*Obitum*	*Obitus*
Genitive	*Obitus*	*Obituum*
Dative	*Obitui*	*Obitibus*
Ablative	*Obitu*	*Obitibus*

How do you separate Second and Fourth Declension nominatives or Third and Fourth Declension dative/ablative plurals?

The answer is in the genitive. Take for example *'Obitus'* and *'Dominus'*. In the genitive form, *'Obitus'* stays as *'Obitus'* but *'Dominus'* becomes *'Domini'*. Those endings then clearly separate the declensions.

Likewise with the dative and ablative plurals, both *'Obitibus'* and *'Patribus'* end in *-ibus*. But using the genitive form of both words will distinguish their declensions: *'Patris'* and *'Obitus'*.

There is, however, one slight exception.

We have, in various chapters, encountered the **irregular Fourth declension noun**, *'Domus'* meaning *'house'*.

Domus, Domus - House

Masculine	Singular	Plural
Nominative	*Domus*	*Domus*
Accusative	*Domum*	*Domos / Domus*
Genitive	*Domus*	*Domuum / Domorum*
Dative	*Domui / Domo*	*Domibus*
Ablative	*Domu / Domo*	*Domibus*

Domus is highly irregular as whilst its endings follow the Fourth Declension, it can also follow the Second Declension – even though *Domus* is feminine.

It may be referred to as a Fourth/Second Declension noun.

Third Declension Adjectives – Part 1

This chapter looks at Third Declension Adjectives. It is split into two parts as Third Declension masculine and feminine forms have one set of endings, and Third Declension neuters have a different set.

A very common 3rd Declension adjective is 'Omnis, Omne' meaning 'all'. The following table shows its endings:

Singular	Masc.	Fem.	Neut.
Nominative	Omnis	Omnis	Omne
Accusative	Omnem	Omnem	Omne
Genitive	Omnis		
Dative	Omni		
Ablative			

Let us compare the two ending forms:

Singular	Noun.	Adj.
Nominative	Various	-is
Accusative	-em	-em
Genitive	-is	-is
Dative	-i	-i
Ablative	-e	-i

As we can see, the accusative, genitive, and dative forms are the same in the singular form. The difference comes with the nominative and ablative endings.

What about the plural endings? Using *Omnis* once again:

Plural	Masc.	Fem.	Neut.
Nominative	*Omnes*	*Omnes*	*Omnia*
Accusative	*Omnes*	*Omnes*	*Omnia*
Genitive	*Omnium*		
Dative	*Omnibus*		
Ablative			

In the plural form, the majority of the endings are the same between genders and cases. How does this compare to 3rd Declension nouns, however?

Plural	Noun.	Adj.
Nominative	*-es*	*-es*
Accusative	*-es*	*-es*
Genitive	*-um*	*-ium*
Dative	*-ibus*	*-ibus*
Ablative	*-ibus*	*-ibus*

Aside from the plural genitive, all the endings are the same.

Omnes is very common in medieval documents as a fair number of charters will begin with the phrase; *"Sciant omnes quod…"*. Legal terminology will be explained later in this book, but this phrase translates to *"Know all men that…"*

Another use of *Omnes* may be to describe an amount, for example, *"omnes terras"* meaning *"all the lands"*. You may come across a sentence which contains *"omne messuagium"*, rather than *"All the messuage"* you can translate it to "the whole message". Thus, *Omne* can mean *all* or *whole*.

Third Declension Adjectives – Part 2

In part one, we see that some 3rd Declension adjectives follow the same ending as the 3rd Declension nouns (with some exceptions). There is, however, another form of the 3rd Declension that is slightly more complex.

The majority of these endings follow the 3rd Declension adjectives, as seen in part 1. **The difference is that there is a stem change** in the same way there is a stem change with 3rd Declension nouns. Let us look at the example of *'Ingens, Ingentis'* meaning *'Huge'*:

Singular	Masc.	Fem.	Neut.
Nominative	*Ingens*	*Ingens*	*Ingens*
Accusative	*Ingentem*	*Ingentem*	*Ingens*
Genitive	*Ingentis*		
Dative	*Ingenti*		
Ablative			

There are a few notable things here. Mainly that this group follows the same stem change and endings as 3rd declension nouns aside from the ablative, which follows the dative.

Singular	**Masc. / Fem.**	**Neuter**
Nominative	*Various*	*Various*
Accusative	*-em*	*Follow Nom.*
Genitive	*-is*	*-is*
Dative	*-i*	*-i*
Ablative	*-e*	*-e*

The plural, however, has the same plural endings as *Omnes* in part 1. The stem, however, will follow the genitive stem.

Plural	Masc.	Fem.	Neut.
Nominative	*Ingentes*	*Ingentes*	*Ingentia*
Accusative	*Ingentes*	*Ingentes*	*Ingentia*
Genitive	*Ingentium*		
Dative	*Ingentibus*		

To know which group a 3rd Declension adjective falls within will dependent upon if there is a **stem change**.

To practice using 3rd Declension adjectives from both groups, here are some sentences to translate:

1. Jacobus concedit omne messuagium cum pertinenciis adiacentibus.

2. Henricus dat existentem domum tribus filiabus.

3. Omnes terre jacent in campo boriali.

4. Gardinum abbutat super viam ex parte orinetali et
   super ripam ex parte australi.

5. Domus pauperis hominis jacet in villa adiacente.

Here are some words to assist you translate:

Adiacens, entis	- *Adjoining*	Pauper, -eris,	- *Poor*
Australis, -e,	- *South*	Orientalis, -e,	- *East*
Borealis, -e,	- *North*	Super	- *On/Upon*

Answers:

1. James grants a whole message with adjacent appurtenances.

2. Henry gives the existing house to the three daughters.

3. All the lands lie in the north field.

4. The garden adjoins the road on the east side and the bank on the south side.

5. The house of the poor man lies in the adjacent town

Prenominal Adjectives – *Alius, Idem, Ipse, Ille, Quidam, Quilibet*

As of now, we have covered the **prenominal pronouns** *qui, que, quod* and *hic, hec, hoc*. There are, however, six other pronominal adjectives that are very common in medieval documents and will greatly expand your vocabulary.

Remember that these adjectives will follow the number, case, and gender of the noun they are connected to.

Although it sounds like a lot, they are straightforward. These six include:

- *Alius, Alia, Alius* – Other
- *Ipse, Ipsa, Ipsum* – Self
- *Idem, Eadem, Idem* – The Same
- *Ille, Illa, Illud* – That, Those
- *Quidam, Quedam, Quoddam* – A Certain
- *Quilibet* – Anyone, Whoever, Whatsoever

This chapter may be a bit lengthy as there are six adjectives to cover but let us waste no time and begin by understanding ***Alius, Alia, Alius*** meaning *Other*.

Singular	Masculine	Feminine	Neuter
Nom.	Alius	Alia	Aliud
Acc.	Alium	Aliam	Aliud
Gen.	Alius	Alius	Alius

Dat.	Alii	Alii	Alii
Abl.	Alio	Alio	Alio
Plural	Masculine	Feminine	Neuter
Nom.	Alii	Alie	Alia
Acc.	Alios	Alias	Alia
Gen.	Aliorum	Aliarum	Aliorum
Dat.	Aliis	Aliis	Aliis
Abl.	Aliis	Aliis	Aliis

Regarding the endings, they are fairly straightforward. What will become clearer as we go on is that many of these adjectives share the same endings and we can see that already by looking at the masculine singular and plural of the genitive case:

- Al**ius**, Ali**orum**
- Hu**ius**, H**orum**
- Cu**ius**, Qu**orum**

Nevertheless, what does *Alius, Alia, Aliud* actually mean? It refers to simply expressing *'another'*. For example, let us take this sentence:

*Dat **aliam** vaccam Domino*

This translates to: *He gives **another** cow to the lord.*

That's all there is to it!

Next, we will take a look at *idem, eadem, idem* meaning 'the same'.

Singular	Masculine	Feminine	Neuter
Nom.	Idem	Eadem	Idem
Acc.	Eundem	Eandem	Idem
Gen.	Euisdem	Euisdem	Euisdem
Dat.	Eidem	Eidem	Eidem
Abl.	Eodem	Eadem	Eodem

Plural	Masculine	Feminine	Neuter
Nom.	Eidem	Eedem	eadem
Acc.	Eosdem	Easdem	Eadem
Gen.	Eorundem	Earundem	Eurundem
Dat.	Eisdem	Eisdem	Eisdem
Abl.	Eisdem	Eisdem	Eisdem

This is an interesting adjective as it contains the pronoun *Is, Ea, Id* – meaning *He, She, It, etc.* This adjective, however, means *the same* and is very common in medieval charters. Here is an example of its use:

*Veniunt ad **eandem** curiam*

This translates to: *They come to **the same** kings court.*

Essentially it is similar to *Predictus* but is used to refer to the same person multiple times. An example in English could be:

*Robert gives a house to Richard. He also gives 3 pennies, a cow, and a messuage with its appurtenances to **the same** Richard.*

Continuing, our next adjective is ***ille, illa, illud*** meaning *that, those.*

Singular	Masculine	Feminine	Neuter
Nom.	Ille	Illa	Illud
Acc.	Illum	Illam	Illud
Gen.	Illius	Illius	Illius
Dat.	Illi	Illi	Illi
Abl.	Illo	Illa	Illo

Plural	Masculine	Feminine	Neuter
Nom.	Illi	Ille	Illa
Acc.	Illos	Illas	Illa
Gen.	Illorum	Illarum	Illorum
Dat.	Illis	Illis	Illis
Abl.	Illis	Illis	Illis

This is a fascinating adjective as has connections to modern European language. As we established back in the first few chapters, Medieval Latin does not have any articles – no words for 'A', or 'The'. When language began to evolve, the need for this became evident. As such the Latin word for one, *unus*, became *'A'* which we know in French as *Un/Une* and in Spanish as *Un/Una* (but don't translate it as *'A'* in Medieval Latin!).

The Latin adjective 'Ille' and 'Illa' would be carved up and used to mean '*The*'. Italian would take the first half, 'il', whilst Spanish would also take 'il' but change the 'i' to an 'e' for 'el'. French would take the second half of *Ille* and *Illa* to get 'le' and 'la'. Oddly enough, Spanish would also take the second half of the accusative masculine plural 'Illos' to get its plural 'Los'.

Though a tangent, it is very interesting to see the evolution of language. For all intents and purposes, however, *Ille, Illa, Illud* in our era means *That, Those*. Here is an example of its use:

*Thomas tenet terras dominis **illius** feodi.*

This translates to: *Thomas holds lands from the lords of **that** fee.*

What is the difference between *hic, hec, hoc* and *ille, illa, illud*? Simply put, **Hic means This/These**, whilst **Ille means That/Those**. Don't get confused!

Let us expand the sentence above to include both adjectives:

*Thomas tenet **has** terras dominis **illius** feodi.*

*Thomas holds **these** lands from the lords of **that** fee.*

Moving on, let us now look at the adjective *ipse, ipsa, ipsum* meaning *self*.

Singular	Masculine	Feminine	Neuter
Nom.	Ipse	Ipsa	Ipsum
Acc.	Ipsum	Ipsam	Ipsum
Gen.	Ipsius	Ipsius	Ipsius
Dat.	Ipsi	Ipsi	Ipsi
Abl.	Ipso	Ipsa	Ipso

Plural	Masculine	Feminine	Neuter
Nom.	Ipsi	Ipse	Ipsa
Acc.	Ipsos	Ipsas	Ipsa
Gen.	Ipsorum	Ipsarum	Ipsorum
Dat.	Ipsis	Ipsis	Ipsis
Abl.	Ipsis	Ipsis	Ipsis

You are probably wondering, what does '*self*' mean? This adjective is referred to as reflexive pronoun and translates as:

- Myself
- Yourself
- Himself, Herself, Itself,
- Ourselves,
- Yourselves
- Themselves

Here is an example of its Latin use:

Ipse Thomas concedit messuagium.

*Thomas, **himself**, grants a messuage.*

This adjective is commonly found at the beginning of a sentence.

This next adjective is very common in medieval documents and is a peculiar word as it is a compound of *qui, que, quod*. What is being referred to is **quidam, quedam, quoddam**, meaning '*a certain*'.

Singular	Masculine	Feminine	Neuter
Nom.	Quidam	Quedam	Quoddam
Acc.	Quendam	Quandam	Quoddam
Gen.	Cuiusdam	Cuiusdam	Cuiusdam
Dat.	Cuidam	Cuidam	Cuidam
Abl.	Quodam	Quodam	Quodam

Plural	Masculine	Feminine	Neuter
Nom.	Quidam	Quedam	Quedam
Acc.	Quosdam	Quasdam	Quedam
Gen.	Quorundam	Quarundam	Quorundam
Dat.	Quibusdam		
Abl.	Quibusdam		

Simply said, this declension is the same as *qui, que, quod*, but with the ending *-dam* slapped on the end.

Quidam, quedam, quoddam is used to refer to a specific person or 'thing' in medieval documents. For example:

*Dant **quasdam** domos filiabus earum.*

*He gives **a certain** gift to his daughters.*

*Thomas concedit **quoddam** messuagium,*

*Thomas grants **a certain** messuage.*

The last adjective we are to cover is **quilibet** meaning *any, whoever, whatsoever, or each*. As with *quidam* it declines like *qui, que, quod* but with -libet as the ending instead of *-dam*.

Singular	Masculine	Feminine	Neuter
Nom.	Quilibet	Quelibet	Quodlibet
Acc.	Quenlibet	Quanlibet	Quodlibet
Gen.	Cuiuslibet	Cuiuslibet	Cuiuslibet
Dat.	Cuilibet	Cuilibet	Cuilibet
Abl.	Quolibet	Quolibet	Quolibet

Plural	Masculine	Feminine	Neuter
Nom.	Quilibet	Quelibet	Quelibet
Acc.	Quoslibet	Quaslibet	Quelibet
Gen.	Quorunlibet	Quarunlibet	Quorunlibet
Dat.	Quibuslibet		
Abl.			

Here is an example of its use:

*Dat acram **cuilibet** filie.*

*He gives an acre to **each** daughter.*

From what I have researched, this adjective is not overly common in Latin as it is a rather vague word (anyone/whoever) whereas the legal documents we are translating prefer absolutes which is why *quidam* is far more frequent. It is, however, worth being aware of, but the key is not to confuse *qui* with *quidam* with *quilibet*.

Now that we have covered all six pronominal adjectives and their declensions, here is a list of sentences that incorporate these adjectives for you to translate:

1. Ipse Henricus concedit easdem terras de hiis dominis illius feodi.

2. Idem Michael filius euisdem Ade tenet quoddam pratum in Norwico.

3. Anna dat quasdam domos filiabus earum.

4. Illa duo messuagia iacent in quadam via in Shepton.

5. Willelmus tenet de alio episcopo et reddit eidem summam duorum solidorum.

6. Quidam Matheus confirmat messuagium quoddam.

7. Galfridus reddit ei duos solidos pro eadem shopa.

8. Sciant omnes quod, ipse Carolus dedi et hac presenti carta confirmavi cuidam Isabelle unum tenementum in Westfelde cum eisdem terris et

predictis pratis adiacentibus nuper in tenura quodam Johannis.

Answers:

1. Henry himself gives the same lands of that fee to these lords.

2. The same Michael, son of the same Adam, holds a certain meadow in Norwich.

3. Anna gives a certain gift to her daughters.

4. Those two messuages lie by a certain road in Shepton.

5. William holds from the other bishop and pays the same sum of two shillings.

6. A certain Matthew confirms a certain messuage.

7. Geoffrey pays him two shillings for the same shop.

8. Know all men that Charles himself gave and confirmed by this present charter one tenement in Westfield to a certain Isabelle with the same lands and adjacent aforesaid meadows recently in tenure by a certain John.

Comparative and Superlative Adjectives

Currently we have used an adjective in direct connection to just one noun, for example: *a whole messuage, the aforesaid land, the ten acres, etc.* This chapter, however, aims to introduce a comparative aspect to the common adjectives we have been using.

You may be confused as to what a superlative and comparative adjective is, but we use these words every day. Quite simply, these are adjectives that have a form which ends in *-er* and *-est* and is used to show a difference or comparison.

Let's look at some examples in English:

- Original Adjective: **Big**
- Comparative Adjective: **Bigger**
- Superlative Adjective: **Biggest**

Sometimes we don't use -er to show a comparison but instead use *more*. For instance, *"The pen is more expensive than the pencil."* Do keep that in mind as when you translate Latin, it still must make sense in English.

I say this as I have seen time and time again, people over thinking how to translate sentences and paragraphs because they try to do it as literal as possible. Latin does not have a word order and it has limited vocabulary, so keep it simple and don't overthink!

Returning to Latin, comparatives and superlatives each have their own ending. By using the example of '*Latus*' meaning '*Wide/Broad*', we can see how this works:

Firstly, **we need the stem of the adjective**, which for *Latus* is *Lat-.*

- Comparative adjectives all have the nominative ending ***-ior*** *(masc. and fem.)* and *-ius* (Neut.)*.*
- Superlative adjectives all have the nominative ending ***-issimus.***

As such, *Latior* means '*Wider*', and *Latissimus* means '*Widest*'.

Most adjectives will follow this standard formular whereby you take the adjective stem and then add on either *-ior, -ius, or -issimus*.

Let us now look at some more adjective examples:

1. *Ingens, Ingentis* – Huge (Stem – *Ingent*)
   - Comparative: **Ingentior**
   - Superlative: **Ingentissimus**

2. *Felix, Felicis* – Happy (Stem – *Felic*)
   - Comparative: **Felicior**
   - Superlative: **Felicissimus**

3. *Miser, Miseri* – Retched (Stem – *Miser*)
   - Comparative: **Miserior**
   - Superlative: **Miserissimus**

4. *Facilis* – Easy (Stem – *Facil*)

- Comparative: **Facilior**
- Superlative: **Facilissimus**

A small number of adjectives that end in *-er* will instead have the superlative ending *-errimus*.

Eger – III (Stem – *Egr*)
- Comparative: **Egrior**
- Superlative: **Egerrimus**

In English as well as Latin, we have irregular comparatives and superlatives that do not follow the rules we have currently outlined.

Two of the most common examples are *Good* and *Bad*. Good does not become *Gooder* and *Goodest*, and Bad does not become *Bader* and *Badest*.

Instead, we have:

- Good, Better, Best
- Bad, Worse, Worst

As such, these are irregular as we have different adjectives to express the comparative and superlative. Latin is the same with these same English examples:

Good	Better	Best
Bonus	*Melior*	*Optimus*

Bad	Worse	Worst
Malus	*Peoir*	*Pessimus*

As a side note, you may notice that the words *Optimus* and *Pessimus* is where we get the terms Optimistic and Pessimistic.

Anywho, there are other irregular examples we should consider:

Big	Bigger	Biggest
Magnus	*Maior*	*Maximus*

Small	Smaller	Smallest
Parvus	*Minor*	*Minimus*

There is no way of simply knowing if an adjective is irregular but that should not matter too much as we are translating from Latin to English.

How do these all these adjectives decline?

- **Comparatives will follow 3rd Declension** adjective endings
- **Superlatives will follow 1st and 2nd Declension** adjective endings.

Here is a table of the comparative adjective declension using *Latus* to help:

Singular	Masculine	Feminine	Neuter
Nom.	Latior	Latior	Latius
Acc.	Latiorem	Latiorem	Latius
Gen.	Latioris	Latioris	Latioris
Dat.	Latiori	Latiori	Latiori
Abl.	Latiore	Latiore	Latiore

Plural	Masculine	Feminine	Neuter
Nom.	Latiores	Latiores	Latiora
Acc.	Latiores	Latiores	Latiora
Gen.	Latiorum		
Dat.	Latioribus		
Abl.			

Returning to the example of *Facilis* – Easy (Stem – *Facil*)

- Comparative: **Facilior**
- Superlative: **Facilissimus**

You may notice from the tables above that in the comparative, *Facilior* follows the 3rd declension and becomes **Faciliorem** in the accusative.

In the superlative, *Facilissimus* follows the 1st and 2nd adjective declension and becomes **Facilissimam**, losing the *-us* and gaining the accusative *-am* ending.

Essentially, take the stem, then add the comparative, then add the case ending. This will tell you all the information you need to know about the adjective.

Translate the following sentences which contain comparative and superlative adjectives (highlighted in bold):

1. **Egerrimus** Galfridus inhabitat **optimum** in villum.

2. **Grossior** Ricardus venit per **faciliorem** viam.

3. Lego **debiliorem** domum fratibus **minoribus** de Lenn.

4. **Justissimus** homo legat summam **ingentissimam pauperrimis** tenetibus.

5. **Augustissimo** et **potentissimo** principi et domino, domino Carolo sexto imperatori, salutem.

Answers:

1. The most ill Geoffrey inhabits the best hospital in the town.

2. The stout Richard comes by the easier road.

3. I bequeath the broken-down house to the lesser brothers of Lenn. *

4. The most justly man bequeaths the most enormous sum to the poorest tenents.

5. To the most august and most powerful prince
    and lord, to the imperial lord Charles VI,
    greetings.

* *'Lesser brothers'* here is used to refer to *Friars*.

Adverbs

In the same way that comparative and superlative adjectives qualify a noun, they can also qualify a verb. Adjectives that do this are called Adverbs.

In English, we categorise adverbs by adjectives that end in -ly and accompany verbs, for example *he ran quickly*. Adverbs can also describe other adjectives, for example, *cautiously fast*.

Adverbs in Latin will end in **-e**, or **-ter**.

Using examples from the previous chapter, here are some adverbs in Latin:

1. *Felix, Felicis* – Happy (Stem – *Felic*)
- Adverb is **Facile** meaning **easily**.

2. Latus – Wide (Stem – *Lat*)
- Adverb is **Late** meaning **broadly**.

3. *Brevis* – Short (Stem – *Brev*)
- Adverb is **Breviter** meaning **briefly**.

Unfortunately, to make things confusing, you can get comparative and superlative adverbs. For comparatives, the ending is **-ius**, and for superlatives the ending is **-issime**.

| *Late* | *Latius* | *Latissime* |
| Wildely | More Widely | Most Widely |

Breviter	*Brevius*	*Brevissime*
Shortly	More Shortly	Most Shortly
Facile	*Facilius*	*Facillime*
Easily	Easier	Easiest

There are, once again, those irregular adverbs. The following is how this decline:

Well	Better	Best
Bone	*Melior*	*Optime*
Badly	Worse	Most Badly
Male	*Pejus*	*Pessime*

Luckily, **adverbs do not decline** as they follow a verb. This means that most adverbs will be given in the dictionary, so you don't need to worry too much about the rules.

Below is an example of an adverb in a sentence:

*Ricardus filius Edwardi et Willelmus venerunt in campo, ubi predictus Hugo fuit in pace domini, et **iniuste** eum insultaverunt.*

Which translates as:

*Richard, son of Edward, and William came into the field where the aforesaid Hugh was in the peace of the lord, and they **unjustly** assaulted him.*

Verbs – Imperfect and Future Tense

We have done a large amount of work on adjectives and nouns thus far aside from looking at the present and perfect tense. At this point, however, all that is really left of this guide is the remaining verb tenses – Future, Imperfect, Future Perfect, Pluperfect, etc.

To remind ourselves, here are the 4 groups of verbs that we have been using to explain the tenses:

Group 1: Confirmo – I Confirm

Group 2: Teneo – I Hold

Group 3: Concedo – I Grant

Group 4: Servio – I Serve

To begin with, let us start by looking at the **imperfect tense**.

What is the imperfect tense? The English language doesn't really have an imperfect tense, rather it can be represented in a few different ways.

- It can be used when **an action is incomplete**, for example: *"I was driving to school when I had an accident."* The task of driving is not completed; therefore, its verb is imperfect.

- It can also be used when there is a **repeated action in the past**, for example: *"When I lived in London, I used to see my friends every week."*

- Lastly, it can be used to **describe a state**, for example: "The window <u>looked</u> on to the beach." Whilst seems similar to the simple past, the window has, and always will, look on to the beach. Therefore, this is describing a state.

It may be a little confusing, but for the purposes of translation, you can more often than not translate the imperfect tense as: "*<Pronoun>* **used to** *<Verb>*".

Using each group as an example:

Group 1: Confirmabam – I used to Confirm

Group 2: Tenebam – I used to Hold

Group 3: Concedebam – I used to Grant

Group 4: Serviebam – I used to Serve

You can clearly see from the verbs above that some of the components within the word have changed between the present and imperfect tenses. There are 3 components of the imperfect:

Stem +   Principal Vowel   +   Ending

Each group has a different principal vowel that is inserted between the stem and ending in the imperfect.

Group 1: -a	*Group 3: -e*
Group 2: -e	*Group 4: -ie*

The stem doesn't change and the endings are all the same for each group.

Here are the imperfect endings:

Imperfect	Group 1	Group 2
I	Confirm-a-**bam**	Ten-e-**bam**
You (s)	Confirma**bas**	Tene**bas**
He/She/It	Confirma**bat**	Tene**bat**
We	Confirma**bamus**	Tene**bamus**
You (pl)	Confirma**batis**	Tene**batis**
They	Confirma**bant**	Tene**bant**

Imperfect	Group 3	Group 4
I	Conced-e-**bam**	Serv-ie-**bam**
You (s)	Concede**bas**	Servie**bas**
He/She/It	Concede**bat**	Servie**bat**
We	Concede**bamus**	Servie**bamus**
You (pl)	Concede**batis**	Servie**batis**
They	Concede**bant**	Servie**bant**

The reason for doing the imperfect first is that the **future tense** also uses these inserted principal vowels. In terms of translation, it is straightforward – either *I will* or *I shall*.

Using each group as an example:

Group 1: Confirmabo – I will Confirm

Group 2: Tenebo – I will Hold

Group 3: Concedam – I will Grant

Group 4: Serviam – I will Serve

Unlike the imperfect, there are some complications with the future tense. Group 1 and 2 share the same endings, as does Group 3 and 4.

Here you can see how it works:

Future	Group 1	Group 2
I	Confirm-a-**bo**	Ten-e-**bo**
You (s)	Confirma**bis**	Tene**bis**
He/She/It	Confirma**bit**	Tene**bit**
We	Confirma**bimus**	Tene**bimus**
You (pl)	Confirma**bitis**	Tene**bitis**
They	Confirma**bunt**	Tene**bunt**

For Group 1 and 2, it's a similar formular to the imperfect tense as you have the stem, inserted vowel, and then the same endings. Group 3 and 4 differ:

Future	Group 3	Group 4
I	Conced-**am**	Servi-**am**
You (s)	Conced**es**	Servi**es**
He/She/It	Conced**et**	Servi**et**
We	Conced**emus**	Servi**emus**
You (pl)	Conced**etis**	Servi**etis**
They	Conced**ent**	Servi**ent**

With these two groups, it follows the imperfect tense formular for all pronouns aside from the 1st Person Singular. Unlike Group 1 and 2, however, these endings are the same as the **Group 2 present tense endings.**

How do you distinguish between a Group 2 Present Verb, and a Group 3 or 4 Future Verb?

The simplest way would be to look in the dictionary or word list for the verb's 1st person singular in the present tense (This is usually given). As we know, Group 2 will end in **-eo** whilst Group 3 will end in **-o**, and Group 4 end in **-io**.

To practice distinguishing between present, imperfect, and future verbs, translate the following and give which tense they ascribe to. Use the word list at the back of this guide and the tables above to help.

Ducam	*Do*	*Legit*
Tenes	*Veniunt*	*Habemus*
Redditis	*Voco*	*Celebratis*
Jacebunt	*Legat*	*Ducent*
Celebras	*Jaceo*	*Confirmabit*
Damus	*Audit*	*Audiebant*
Edificabunt	*Monent*	*Leget*
Monebam	*Edificamus*	*Vocabat*
Dimittet	*Ducemus*	*Regemus*

* The answers are on the following page

ANSWERS:

Ducam – Future, I will lead

Tenes – Present, You (s) hold

Redditis – Present, You (pl) play

Jacebunt – Future, They will lie

Celebras – Present, You (s) celebrate

Damus – Present, We give

Edificabunt – Future, They will build

Monebam – Imperfect, I used to warn

Dimittet – Future, He/She/It will dismiss

Do – Present, I give

Veniunt – Present, They come

Voco – Present, I call

Legat – Present, He/She/It bequeaths

Jaceo – Present, I lie

Audit – Present, He hears

Monent – Present, They warn

Edificamus – Present, We build

Ducemus – Future, We will lead

Legit – Present, He/She/It reads

Habemus – Present, We have

Celebratis – Present, You (pl) celebrate

Ducent – Present, They lead

Confirmabit – Future, He/She/It will confirm

Audiebant – Imperfect, They used to hear

Leget – Future, He/She/It will read

Vocabat - Imperfect, He/She/It used to call

Regemus – Future, We will rule

Verbs – Future Perfect and Pluperfect

Continuing our advancement on verbs, we are moving on towards two new tenses which are fairly uncommon in English but are used widely in medieval charters. Built off the perfect tense stem, these two tenses are the future perfect and pluperfect.

Looking at the future perfect to begin with, this is a verb tense that we don't have in English as we would tend to use the present tense instead. This tense, however, can be deployed in two ways:

1. To express completed action in the future.
   "*I shall have eaten by tonight*"
2. To express when something is likely.
   "*In Paris you would have seen the Eifel Tower*"

Medieval Latin tends to follow the first of these uses and can be found primarily at the beginning of a charter:

"*To whom these charters shall have confirmed…*"

The good news with the future perfect tense is that all the endings are the same across conjugations. All that changes is the stem as it uses the stem of the perfect tense. Here is a recap of the stem changes for each conjugation:

	Present	**Perfect**
Group 1	*Confirm-*	*Confirmav-*
Group 2	*Ten-*	*Tenu-*
Group 3	*Conced-*	*Concess-*
Group 4	*Serv-*	*Serviv-*

With that in mind, here are the future perfect endings:

Future Perfect	Group 1	Group 2
I	Confirmav–**ero**	Tenu–**ero**
You (s)	Confirmav–**eris**	Tenu–**eris**
He/She/It	Confirmav–**erit**	Tenu–**erit**
We	Confirmav–**erimus**	Tenu–**erimus**
You (pl)	Confirmav–**eristis**	Tenu–**eristis**
They	Confirmav–**erint**	Tenu–**erint**

Future Perfect	Group 3	Group 4
I	Concess–**ero**	Serviv–**ero**
You (s)	Concess–**eris**	Serviv–**eris**
He/She/It	Concess–**erit**	Serviv–**erit**
We	Concess–**erimus**	Serviv–**erimus**
You (pl)	Concess–**eristis**	Serviv–**eristis**
They	Concess–**erint**	Serviv–**erint**

We would translate the future perfect tense as "*I shall have ___*", for example:

- *Confirmero* – I shall have confirmed
- *Tenuero* – I shall have held
- *Concessero* – I shall have granted
- *Servivero* – I shall have served

For irregular verbs such as *concedo*, do not worry as many dictionaries will give you the perfect stem along with the present so you can identify the word you are searching for.

Next, we will look at the tense known as the Pluperfect. This tense is used to express a something further back in time than the simple past tense. For example: "*I had called before I left the home*"

In this sentence we have two past tenses but the first (*I had called*) happens before the following event. As such it is expressed as the pluperfect tense.

Like the future perfect, the pluperfect also takes the perfect stem and shares the same verb endings across all conjugation groups.

Pluperfect	Group 1	Group 2
I	Confirmav–**eram**	Tenu–**eram**
You (s)	Confirmav–**eras**	Tenu–**eras**
He/She/It	Confirmav–**erat**	Tenu–**erat**
We	Confirmav–**eramus**	Tenu–**eramus**
You (pl)	Confirmav–**eratis**	Tenu–**eratis**
They	Confirmav–**erant**	Tenu–**erant**

Pluperfect	Group 3	Group 4
I	Concess–**eram**	Serviv–**eram**
You (s)	Concess–**eras**	Serviv–**eras**
He/She/It	Concess–**erat**	Serviv–**erat**
We	Concess–**eramus**	Serviv–**eramus**
You (pl)	Concess–**eratis**	Serviv–**eratis**
They	Concess–**erant**	Serviv–**erant**

You would translate these by saying *"I had __"*, for example: *Confirmaveram* – I had confirmed.

Past, Present, and Future Participles (Supine)

Dictionaries and word lists give four principal parts to each verb:

- *Confirmo* – 1st Person Present
- *Confirmare* – Infinitive
- *Confirmavi* – 1st Person Perfect
- *Confirmatum* – Supine (Participles)

In a dictionary/word list, this could be abbreviated and expressed as: *Concedo, -ere, -cessi, -cessum*

So, what is the supine? Essentially, it is **a verb which behaves like an adjective and agrees with a noun.** In English, this is often expressed by a verb that has *-ing* or *-ed* on the end, such as "*The laughing man*."

It is worth noting that in Medieval Latin, the supine is quite rare but is often found at the very beginning of charters, or at the very end.

The **Past Participle** is a verbal-adjective that is expressed, in English, by the simple past *(-ed),* such as "*called*". Many verbs, such as *called*, are known as 'weak verbs' as their form does not change between the simple past and the past participle. Other verbs, known as 'strong verbs', do change their form.

Here are a few examples (*Present – Past – Participle*):

- Drink – Drank – Drunk
- Sing – Sang – Sung
- Lie – Lay – Lain

If you are unsure how to express a participle, imagine saying "I have __" as the answer will be the participle form. *"I have drank"* does not make grammatical sense, whereas *"I have drunk"* does!

In Latin, the past prticiple has a form for each conjugation:

- 1st Conjugation: *present stem* + *-atum*
- 2nd Conjugation: *present stem* + *-itum*
- 3rd Conjugation: *Irregular*
- 4th Conjugation: *present stem* + *-itum*

For irregular supine verbs, their stem will be given in the dictionary or word list. However, now we have our supine stems, we can look at how they decline.

Participles follow the noun they are associated with in number, case, and gender. Additionally, **past participles will decline like *Predictus* (1st and 2nd Declension adjective endings).**

In terms of translation, you can write it the same way you would the simple past or "*having been ___*". In the case of **confirmatum**, it would translate to either "*confirmed*" or "*having been confirmed*" – the choice is yours.

The following is a Latin example of the past participle:

1. Messuagium abbuttat super pontem **emendatum** filiis meis.

- *The messuage borders upon the bridge **repaired** by my sons.*
- Or, *The messuage borders upon the bridge **having been repaired** by my sons.*

Notice that **emendatum** complements and follows **pontem** in number, case, and gender – this is very important to look for.

Translate these other sentences:

2. Hec est carta confirmata patri meo.

3. Tenet terras datas domina.

4. Domus concessa mee filie iacet in Briggegate.

5. Terre tente Anna iacent in campo.

6. Hoc est testamentum conditum Roberto.

7. Johannes concedit tres acras terre iacentes in campo vocato Grenefeld.

Answers:

2. This is a charter confirmed to my father.

3. He holds lands given by the Lady.

4. The house granted to my daughter lies in Briggegate.

5. The lands lie in the field.

6. This is a will made by Robert.

7. John grants three acres of land lying in a field called Grenefeld.

The final question above contains a red herring - '*Iacentes*' does not fit any verb endings we have covered because, in this context, it is a **present participle**.

Present participles are very straightforward as these will translate as verbs ending in -*ing*. Whilst past participles follow the endings of 1st and 2nd declension adjectives

(*Predictus*), **the present participle adopts the second part of the 3rd Declension (*Ingens, Ingentis*).**

Also like the past, the present participle has a form for each conjugation:

- 1st Conjugation: *present stem* + *-ans (sing.) / antis (pl.)*
- 2nd Conjugation: *present stem* + *-ens/-entis*
- 3rd Conjugation: *present stem* + *-ens/ -entis*
- 4th Conjugation: *present stem* + *-iens/ -ientis*

Returning to the question above, '*iaceo*' is a 2nd Conjugation verb meaning the stem (i*ac*-) takes on the plural form (-entis) to become the present participle iacentis.

In the question, *iacentes* follows *acras* in the sentence which is feminine, accusative, and plural. Using the adjective grammar sheet, the Fem. Acc. Pl. of *Ingens* is *Ingentes*. This means that *iacentis* becomes *iacentes*.

The key is to keep in mind the most important lesson of Latin: Words have to agree in case, gender and noun. If you have a complex word such as *confirmantibus* and are unsure how to translate it, look for the word it is paired with, look at its number, case and gender, and work back from there.

It is a matter of deduction:

Confirmantibus

- *Confirmantibus* is a 1st Conjugation verb
- It is taking the 3rd declension ending rather than the 1st and 2nd meaning it is a present participle.
- The -*antibus* ending means the participle is definitely plural but could be any case or gender – as such, look at the context.

It is that simple and this is a technique that, as texts get more complex, you continuously reapply. Medieval Latin is nothing but a puzzle, and you are simply putting the pieces together.

Lastly, we have the **future participle**. Unlike the previous two participles, the future does not have an equivalent in English. Instead, we would translate this as "*about to __*", "*in order to __*" or, "*prepared to ___*".

The future participle is very common at the beginning of charters as a frequent theme is to address a crowd:

"*Omnibus Christi fidelibus hoc presens cartum* **visuris** *et* **audituris**..."

"To all the faithful of Christ **about to see** and **about to hear** this present charter..."

The future participle also follows the 1st and 2nd Declension Adjective endings, but there is a change in the stem.

Essentially, you take the stem of the supine (confirm**atum**) and **replace it with -urus, -ura, -urum** (confirm**urus**). This is the same for all conjugations.

- *Video* is an irregular, 2nd Conjugation verb meaning *to see*. Its supine is *Visum*, thus its future participle is visurus (-a, -um).

- *Do* is our infamous 1st Conjugation verb, meaning *to give*. Its supine is *Datum* and therefore its future participle is *Daturus (-a, -um)*.

- *Concedo* is a 3rd Conjugation verb, meaning *to grant*. Its supine is *Concessum*, thus its future participle is *Concessurus (-a, -um)*.

Like all participles, its ending will then complement the number, case, and ending of the word the participle is following.

Direct and Reported Speech in Charters

Throughout this guide we have been looking at examples of direct speech. Charters, however, can also be constructed using reported / indirect speech.

Firstly, before we dive into the deep end of infinitives, what is direct and reported speech?

Direct speech is when something is recalled, explained, or spoken about by someone part of that scenario. For example:

- Jane is going shopping
- I work at a bank
- Paul is hungry

Reported speech, however, is the act of speaking about a scenario you are not part of, and so you use indirect language. For example:

- John says that Jane is going shopping
- They say that they are cold
- He said he had a new car

In terms of charters, one written in direct speech will use nominatives, personal pronouns, and verbs – as we have seen. A charter using reported speech, however, will see certain changes to those nominatives, verbs, and personal pronouns to make the language indirect.

Medieval Latin expresses indirect speech in two ways:

1. A Non-Classical Latin Construction

This is the simplest way to express indirect speech.

Take this sentence: *"Willelmus dat tres acras terre Roberto"*. In Medieval Latin, "Sciant Omnes Quod" is used as an indirect statement to make the sentence reported speech.

"Sciant omnes quod Willelmus dat tres acras terre Roberto."

Quite simply, charters and documents were written to be read aloud which is why these charter statements and the use of reported speech were deployed.

2. A Classical Latin Construction

This is one of the few rarities in which Medieval and Classical Latin overlap. Rather than inserting an indirect speech prefix, this aims to change the sentence as a whole to fit the indirect form.

Let us return to the sentence: *"Sciant omnes quod Willelmus dat tres acras terre Roberto."*

Using the classical Latin construction, this sentence would become:

"Sciant omnes Willelmum dare tres acras terre Roberto."

Three things have changed which defines this form:

1. The removal of *Quod*
2. The nominative (*Willelmus*) becomes accusative (*Willelmum*)
3. The verb (Dat) becomes an infinitive (Dare)

To understand how this changes the sentence, let us look at how this is expressed in English. Look at the following example:

"I know that he is an honourable man"

When changed to indirect speech it becomes:

"I know <u>him</u> <u>to be</u> an honourable man"

Just as we have done in Latin, we have removed *'that'*, changed the nominative (*he*) to an accusative (*him*), and changed the verb (*is*) into an infinitive (*to be*).

Whilst on the topic, what is the infinitive and how do you find it?

The infinitive is form of a verb that isn't ascribed to a pronoun. It is instead expressed as "*To __*" ie. To be, to confirm, to grant, and so on.

If we remember back to the previous chapter, it was mentioned that dictionaries and word lists give four principal parts to each verb:

- *Confirmo* – 1st Person Present
- *Confirmare* – Infinitive
- *Confirmavi* – 1st Person Perfect
- *Confirmatum* – Supine (Participles)

As you can see, the 2nd principal part is the infinitive. As such, if you ever see a verb with an unfamiliar ending, look it up at the back of this guide and its forms are given.

Each conjugation has its own **present infinitive** ending:

- 1st Conjugation: *present stem + **-are***
- 2nd Conjugation: *present stem + **-ere***
- 3rd Conjugation: *present stem + **-ere***
- 4th Conjugation: *present stem + **-ire***

There are, however, also **perfect infinitive endings** for past tense verbs that change in indirect speech:

- 1st Conjugation: *perfect stem + **-isse***
- 2nd Conjugation: *perfect stem + **-isse***
- 3rd Conjugation: *perfect stem + **-isse***
- 4th Conjugation: *perfect stem + **-isse***

Using all this, here is an exercise in which you will have to turn a sentence in the direct form into the indirect present, and then into the indirect perfect (using Classical Latin Construction).

The first one below is completed as an example:

Original: *Willelmus Broune dicit quod Ricardus filius suus concedit predictas terras ecclesie Sancti Barnabe*

Translated: William says that Richard, his son, grants the aforesaid lands to the church of St. Barnabas.

Present Indirect: *Willelmus Broune dicit Ricardum filium suum concedere predictas terras ecclesie Sancti Barnabe.*

Perfect Indirect: *Willelmus Broune dicit Ricardum filium suum concessisse* predictas terras ecclesie Sancti Barnabe.*

*Note that concedit would adopt the perfect stem to become concessit (concessisse in the perfect infinitive). Don't skip a step and just think it would be concedisse!

Remember that the words still have to agree which is why *filius suus* becomes *filium suum* when *Ricardus* becomes *Ricardum*.

Try converting the following sentence yourself:

Sciant omnes quod nos Robertus et Alicia uxor mea damus et hac carta confirmamus tria prata Emme et Marie filiabus nostris.

Answer:

Original: *Sciant omnes quod nos Robertus et Alicia uxor mea damus et hac carta confirmamus tria prata Emme et Marie filiabus nostris.*

Translation: Know all that we, Robert and Alice, my wife, have given and by this charter confirmed three meadows to Emma and Mary our daughters.

Present Indirect: *Sciant omnes nos Robertum et Aliciam uxorem meam dare et hac carta confirmare tria prata Emme et Marie filiabus nostris.*

Perfect Indirect: *Sciant omnes nos Robertum et Aliciam uxorem meam dedisse et hac carta confirmavisee* tria prata Emme et Marie filiabus nostris.*

*Sometimes in charters, *confirmavisse* will be abbreviated to *confirmasse* to make its length manageable.

Note that the content hasn't changed, only the form. This is crucial if you come across this in a charter as you should not translate it literally. Whether direct or indirect, the meaning is the same – **the purpose of this chapter is merely to recognise that this structure of charters exists**.

The following sentences are a little more complex in language but by using the word list and grammar sheets, they can be completed with ease.

Translate the following sentences that follow the *Classical Latin Construction*:

1. Sciant omnes me Gilbertum Waleys dedisse, concessisse et hac carta mea confirmasse monachis abbatie Sancti Johannis Baptiste tres messuagia que habebam ex dono domini Willelmi Howard.

2. Pateat (*Let it be known*) omnibus presentibus et futuris nos unanimi assensu et voluntate ordinasse, fecisse et constituisse loco nostro attornatos nostros dilectos in Christo Henricum le Espicer et Johannem de Bradeston.

3. Andreas dicit se tres messuagia ecclesie Sancti Barnabe dare.

4. Notum sit (*Be it known*) me prefatum Henricum remisisse totum ius meum in illis terris.

5. Sciant omnes presents et future ad quos presents littere pervenerint nos Willelmum Godwin et Aliciam uxorum meam dare, concedere, et hac presenti carta confirmare Ricardo Grene unum tenementum cum omnibus suis pertinenciis.

6. Noveritis (*Know*) me Matildam in pura viduetate mea concessisse, relaxasse, et omnino quietumclamasse Ade filio meo et heredibus suis totum ius meum vel clamium quod habui nomine dotis in omnibus terris et tenementis quibuscumque, que sunt dicti Ade filii mei die confeccionis huius scripti.

7. Predicti Adam et Agnes uxor eius recognoverunt predicta tenementa cum pertinenciis esse ius ipsius Willelmi.

8. Dicit quod habuit cartam manumissionis domini Abbatis et clamat se esse liberum hominem.

Answers:

1. Know all men that I, Gilbert Waleys, gave, granted, and confirmed by this my charter to the monks of the abbey of Saint John the Baptiste three messuages that I used to have from a gift of William Howard.

2. Let it be known to all present and future that we by unanimous assent and will have appointed, made and established in our place our attorneys beloved in Christ, Henry le Espicer and John of Bradeston.
3. Andrew says that he is giving three messuages to the church of St Barnabas.

4. Be it known that I the aforesaid Henry have remised all my rights to those lands.

5. Know all men present and future to whom these present letters have arrived, that we William Godwin and Alice, my wife, gave, granted, and confirmed by this present charter to Richard Grene one tenement with its whole appurtenances.

6. Know that I, Matilda, in my pure widowhood granted, released, and quitclaimed in every way to Adam, my son and all his heirs, my right or claim which I had in the name of dowry for all the lands and tenements whatsoever, which are of the said Adam my son on the day of the making of this writing.

7. The aforesaid Adam and Agnes, his wife, acknowledged the aforesaid tenements with its appurtenances to be the right of William himself.

8. He says that he had a charter of manumission of the lord Abbot and claims he is a free man.

Irregular Verbs – To Be

In all modern foreign languages, the verb '*To Be*' is renowned as the ultimate irregular verb. Latin is no different. This chapter is more about the recognition of the verb as its use will be explored further in the following *Passive Verb* chapter.

With that in mind, let us look at the Latin declension:

Sum, esse, fui – To Be

Present	Future	Imperfect
sum	*ero*	*eram*
es	*eris*	*eras*
est	*erit*	*erat*
sumus	*erimus*	*eramus*
estis	*eritis*	*eratis*
sunt	*erunt*	*erant*
Perfect	**Future Perfect**	**Pluperfect**
fui	*fuero*	*fueram*
fuisti	*fueris*	*fueras*
fuit	*fuerit*	*fuerat*
fuimus	*fuerimus*	*fueramus*
fuistis	*fueritis*	*fueratis*
fuerunt	*fuerint*	*fuerant*

Infinitive:
- Present: Esse
- Perfect: Fuisse

- Future: Futurus, -a, -um

In terms of translation, it should be fairly straightforward. Remember, however, that English is equally as irregular (*am, is, was, were, will be, having been, etc*).

The present, future, and imperfect tense of verb '*To Be*' is also used directly by the verb 'To Be Able'. This verb is notable because it will always be followed be an infinitive (To be able **to** ___).

Possum, posse, potui – To Be Able

Present	Future	Imperfect
possum	potero	poteram
potes	poteris	poteras
potest	poterit	poterat
possumus	poterimus	poteramus
potestis	poteritis	poteratis
possunt	poterunt	poterant
Perfect	**Future Perfect**	**Pluperfect**
potui	potuero	potueram
potuisti	potueris	potueras
potuit	potuerit	poterat
potuimus	potuerimus	poteramus
potuistis	potueritis	potueratis

Infinitive:
- Present: Posse
- Perfect: Potuisse
- Future: Potens, Potentis

94

What you may notice is that the perfect, future perfect, and pluperfect follow the same 2nd Declension verb endings.

The following verb, *Eo – To Go*, is classed as a compound verb. Usually, the following verb is attached as a suffix to another verb. It is unlikely to find this verb on its own.

Eo, Ire, Ivi, Itum – To Go

Present	Future	Imperfect
eo	ibo	ibam
is	ibis	ibas
it	ibit	ibat
imus	ibimus	ibamus
itis	ibitis	ibatis
eunt	ibunt	ibant
Perfect	**Future Perfect**	**Pluperfect**
ivi	ivero	iveram
ivisti	iveris	iveras
ivit	iverit	iverat
ivimus	iverimus	iveramus
ivistis	iveritis	iveratis
iverunt	iverint	iverant

Infinitive:
- Present: Ire
- Perfect: Isse
- Future: iturus, -a, -um, esse

95

So, how does this verb work as a compound? Here are some examples of its use:

- Trans**eo** – I go across (Where we get the word **transit**)
- Per**eo** – I pass/die
- Ex**eo** – I go out (Also where we get the word **exit**)

Note that you can come across declensions of *To Go* that leave out the *'v'*. This is especially common with compound verbs such as **Transiit** *rather than* **Transivit**.

Eo is not the only verb that is a commonly used in as compound. **Facco** (*facco, facere, faci, factum*) for example, meaning *To Do/Make,* can be expressed as the compound **conficio** meaning *To Confect*.

Another is **Fero** (*fero, ferre, tuli, latum*) which is highly irregular but means *To Carry*. The issue with highly irregular verbs like fero is that they can easily trip people up.

If you were unfamiliar with the verb **Contulit** (a compound of *Fero* meaning To Confer), you may think it was 4th Conjugation as it ends in *-it* and its first-person present would thus be **Contulio**. This, of course, is wrong as the first-person present is **Confero**.

More often than not, if a word contains a form of *tulit* then it's a compound of *Fero*. A very common example

in pipe rolls is **Abstulit** which, in the first-person, is
Aufero meaning *To Steal.*

Faco and Fero, however, decline the same way as
another important verb – **Capio** (*Capio, Capere, Cepi,
Captum*) – *To Take.*

Here is its conjugation:

Present	Future	Imperfect
Capio	Capiam	Capiebam
Capis	Capies	Capiebas
Capit	Capiet	Capiebat
Capimus	Capiemus	Capiebamus
Capitis	Capietis	Capiebatis
Capiunt	Capient	Capiebant
Perfect	**Future Perfect**	**Pluperfect**
In the perfect, future perfect, and pluperfect, these verbs follow regular 3rd Conjugation endings.		

Infinitive:
- Present: Capi
- Perfect: Captus fuisse
- Future: Captus fore

To consolidate this chapter, all these irregular verbs are
really only to be recognised. Quite simply, use the
grammar sheet and word list to translate them. The
most important irregular verb, however, is the verb *To*

Be as this is incorporated within Passive Verbs in the following chapter.

Passive Verbs

Thus far we have been solely concentrating on Active verbs. This chapter, however, is to introduce the passive which, though more uncommon, is just as important. To understand what the difference between the Active and Passive is, let us firstly look at it in English:

The dog chased the cat

In this sentence the subject (dog) is doing an action to the object (cat). The verb (chased) in this sense is an active verb because the subject noun is doing an action.

Let us then contemplate this sentence:

The cat was chased by the dog

The cat in this sentence is now the subject and the dog is now the object. The verb has changed too as it is now accompanied by the auxiliary word *'was' and* is doing its action to the subject.

When the action of the verb is to the subject rather than by the subject, the verb is passive.

In English, to form the Passive we use the verb '*To Be'* with a past participle. For example, "*he was chased"* or, "*it was agreed that".*

Latin, unfortunately, is not as simple and straightforward. Arguably the passive present is loosely formed from the active present:

ACTIVE Present	PASSIVE Present
Confirmo	Confirmor
Confirmas	Confirmaris
Confirmat	Confirmatur
Confirmamus	Confirmamur
Confirmatis	Confirmamini
Confirmant	Confirmantur

This is seen clearer in the 3rd person whereby the active -at ending evolves to include the addition of *ur* to get the passive -atur.

Comparing the 3rd person active and passive from the imperfect, and future tenses yields similar comparisons:

- Confirm**abit** (future active), Confirm**abitur** (passive)
- Confirm**abat** (imperfect active), Confirm**abatur** (passive)

Its noteworthy to know that the 2nd person passive is highly uncommon but it emerges from the infinitive:

- Comfirm**are** (inf.), Confirm**aris** (passive)

You can sort of see where the passive emerges from but how does it conjugate? Luckily the passive endings are the same for conjugation groups 1 and 2, and likewise for 3 and 4.

The only thing to note is that the inserted vowel will change between conjugations as covered in previous chapters.

Passive endings for group 1 and 2:

PASSIVE Indicative		
Present – **I Confirm**	**Imperfect –** **I used to be** **Confirmed**	**Future –** **I will be** **Confirmed**
Confirm**or** (I)	Confirma**bar**	Confirma**bor**
Confirm**aris** (You s.)	Confirma**baris**	Confirma**beris**
Confirm**atur** (He/She/It)	Confirma**batur**	Confirma**bitur**
Confirm**amur** (We)	Confirma**bamur**	Confirma**bimur**
Confirm**amini** (You pl.)	Confirma**bamini**	Confirma**bimini**
Confirm**antur** (They)	Confirma**bantur**	Confirma**buntur**
Perfect – I was **Confirmed**	**Future Perfect – I** **shall have been** **Confirmed**	**Pluperfect – I** **had been Called**
Confirm**atus, a, um** **fui**	Confirm**atus** **fuero**	Confirm**atus** **fueram**
Confirm**atus fuisti**	Confirm**atus** **fueris**	Confirm**atus** **fueras**
Confirm**atus fuit**	Confirm**atus** **fuerit**	Confirm**atus** **fuerat**
Confirm**ati, e, a** **fuimus**	Confirm**ati** **fuerimus**	Confirm**ati** **fueramus**
Confirm**ati fuistis**	Confirm**ati** **fueritis**	Confirm**ati** **fueratis**
Confirm**ati fuerunt**	Confirm**ati fuerint**	Confirm**ati** **fuerant**

Passive endings for group 3 and 4:

PASSIVE Indicative		
Present – I Grant	**Imperfect – I used to be Granted**	**Future – I will be Granted**
Concedor (I)	*Concedebar*	*Concedar*
Concederis (You s.)	*Concedebaris*	*Concederis*
Conceditur (He/She/It)	*Concedebatur*	*Concedetur*
Concedimur (We)	*Concedebamur*	*Concedemur*
Concedimini (You pl.)	*Concedebamini*	*Concedemini*
Conceduntur (They)	*Concedebantur*	*Concedentur*
Perfect – I was Granted	**Future Perfect – I shall have been Granted**	**Pluperfect – I had been Granted**
Concessus, a, um fui	*Concessus fuero*	*Concessus fueram*
Concessus fuisti	*Concessus fueris*	*Concessus fueras*
Concessus fuit	*Concessus fuerit*	*Concessus fuerat*
Concessi, e, a fuimus	*Concessi fuerimus*	*Concessi fueramus*
Concessi fuistis	*Concessi fueritis*	*Concessi fueratis*
Concessi fuerunt	*Concessi fuerint*	*Concessi fuerant*

What you may have noticed by the declensions is that the **perfect, future perfect, and pluperfect** are very similar to English as they in that they incorporate the verb "To Be".

Whilst in English we use the *'To Be'* verb + past participle, Latin merely swaps this around and expresses the passive by the **past participle + irregular verb**. For example: *Confirmatus fui*

The past participle also agrees in gender with and number with the context it refers to:

- The singular: *Confirmatus, -a, -um*
- The plural: *Confirmati, -e, -a*

This is where English and Latin diverge as in English, we don't know whether the passive is plural or singular or feminine or masculine without context:

Robert **was challenged** by advanced mathematics

'Robert' provides the gender and number context to the passive verb. Latin, however, expresses this by the verb itself.

'Was Challenged' in this context would be expressed as **Calumniatus fuit**, and if the context was feminine, it would be *Calumniata fuit*. Neuter, however, is an unlikely passive verb.

The perfect, future perfect, and pluperfect tenses, however, are not the only ones to incorporate the verb 'To Be'.

During the medieval era, especially in the later centuries, language was evolving into a form more familiar with today than the ancient world. As such, the passive present tense can be found in charters to have an alternative form that uses the present tense of *Sum*.

Present Passive	Alternative Form
Confirmor (I)	Confirm**atus**, (-a, -um) **sum**
Confirmaris (You s.)	Confirm**atus es**
Confirmatur (He/She/It)	Confirm**atus est**
Confirmamur (We)	Confirmati (-e, -a) **sumus**
Confirmamini (You pl.)	Confirmati **estis**
Confirmantur (They)	Confirmati **sunt**

The translation is the same but just be aware that this may pop up in a later medieval charter.

Passives, like active verbs, also have an **infinitive** for each conjugation:

- Confirmari – to be confirmed
- Teneri – to be held
- Concedi – to be granted
- Serviri – to be served

Using the grammar sheets and word list, translate the following sentences containing passive verbs:

1. Illa tenementa tenebantur Roberto.

2. Acra in campo boriali confirmabitur Johanni.

3. Messuagium jacet in strate, que vocatur Overton.

4. Warantizabimus dictam terram Henrico, ut predictam est.

5. Tres solidi redditi fuerant domino.

6. Jana uxor Galfridi examinate fuit senescallo.

7. Pecia terre septa est heredibus domini.

8. Preceptum fuit distringere Johannem Broun pro sua defalta.

9. Candele date fuerunt ecclesie vicario.

10. Sciatis me teneri Simo Styward in tribus libris.

11. Lego dimidiam marcam ecclesie quam reparari feci.

Answers:

1. Those tenements used to be held by Robert.

2. The acre in the north field shall be confirmed to John.

3. The messuage lies in the road, which is called Overton.

4. We shall warrant the aforesaid land to Henry, as is aforesaid.

5. Three shillings had been paid to the Lord.

6. Jane, the wife of Geoffrey, was examined by the steward.

7. A portion of land is enclosed by the heirs of the lord.

8. It is ordered to distrain John Broun for his defection.

Gerunds and Gerundives

The crusade on verbs continues with gerunds (**verbal nouns)** and gerundives (**verbal adjectives**).

In English, a **gerund** is represented by adding *–ing* to the verb, similar to the present participle. For example:

I like <u>running</u>.

In other words, a gerund expresses the idea or concept of a verb in the form of a noun. In Latin gerunds are **2nd Declension neuter nouns and decline like messuagium**.

Gerunds are also **formed from the present participle**, which you will remember are third declension adjectives and decline like *ingens* (see the adjective grammar sheet).

Here is a table to show what each verb conjugation looks like in the gerund form:

1st Person Present	Present Participle	Gerund
(1) Confirmo	*Confirmans*	*Confirmandum*
(2) Teneo	*Tenens*	*Tenendum*
(3) Concedo	*Concedens*	*Concedum*
(4) Servio	*Serviens*	*Serviendum*

You will see that the gerund is formed by removing the final '*-s*' of the present participle and adding '*-dum*'.

So, when is a gerund usually used? It is most commonly found in the following cases:

1. <u>In the Accusative:</u>

This is to **express purpose** and can often best be translated into English by an infinitive:

*Ibo in bibliothecam **ad legendum** librum.*
*I shall go to the library **to read** (ie in order to read) a book.*

2. <u>As a Genitive:</u>

*Ars scriben**di**, meaning, The art **of writing***

*Modus operan**di**, meaning, The way (or method) **of working***

3. <u>In the Ablative:</u>

*Discimus legen**do**, meaning, We learn **by reading***

Hopefully from this you should see that the translation of the gerund is fairly straightforward. The main tip is merely the recognition that the word is a verb and not a noun.

For ease of access, here are all the endings for the gerund form using *Confirmo*:

Gerund Endings	
Accusative	Confirm**andum**
Genitive	Confirm**andi**
Dative	Confirm**ando**
Ablative	Confirm**ando**

Often gerunds are accompanied by a preposition which slightly changes their meaning:

Case	Preposition	Gerund
Accusative	**ad**	Confirm**andum**
Genitive	**causa**	Confirm**andi**
Dative	**-**	Confirm**ando**
Ablative	**ab, de, ex, in, pro**	Confirm**ando**

The meanings to all of these propositions can be found in the word list at the back of this guide.

A gerundive is a verbal adjective. It is formed in the same way as a gerund, but has adjectival endings, i.e., it has masculine, feminine and neuter endings and declines like *Predictus*.

1st Person Present	Gerund	Gerundives
(1) Confirmo	*Confirmandum*	*Confirmandus, -a, -um*
(2) Teneo	*Tenendum*	*Tenendus, -a, -um*
(3) Concedo	*Concedum*	*Concedus, -a, -um*
(4) Servio	*Serviendum*	*Serviendus, -a, -um*

In terms of translation, English doesn't have an equivalent but should be translated as *"To Be" + Past Participle.*

Essentially it carries the meaning of something that is worthy or ought to be done and can be a way of expressing the English '*must*', especially when used with the verb to be (*sum*). As a general rule, however, you can translate the gerundive as *'to be done'* implying some form of obligation.

*Hic puer **vocandus** est Johannes*

*This boy **is to be called** John,* or, *This boy **shall (must) be called** John.*

A highly common gerundive found in charters is *habendum et tenendum* which literally means, 'To be had and to be held.' A better way to translate the phrase whenever and however it occurs is '***To have and to hold'.***

It is also usually followed by the dative case: *to have and to hold a piece of land **to** someone.*

To complicate things, gerunds are active in meaning and sometimes take an object. For example: "*Ibo in bibliothecam ad legendum librum*" means I shall go to the library to read a book, where *'book'* is the object of *'to read'*.

Sometimes instead of a gerund taking an object, a gerundive is used. Here is an example of this:

*Simo fecit finem domino ijs. pro hac convencione **confirmanda**.*

*Simon made fine to the lord of two shillings in return for **confirming** this agreement.*

Here *'convencione'* is in the ablative case after *'pro'* and the gerundive agrees with it in the **ablative, feminine, singular,** *confirmanda.*

This literally means *'in return for the agreement to-be-confirmed'*. As above, translate the gerundive as a gerund taking an object *'in return for confirming this agreement'*.

Try translating the following gerund and gerundive sentences:

<u>Gerunds</u>

1. Item lego ad distribuendum inter leprosos Norwici xld.

2. Petrus de Nerford attachiatus fuit ad respondendum Ricardo filio Turkili.

3. Tenet tenementum faciendo xii aruras per annum.

4. Commendo corpus meum ad sepelliendum in ecclesia Sancti Georgii.

5. Reddendo inde annuatim prefato Willelmo et assignatis suis unam rubeam rosam ad festum nativitatis sancti Johannis Baptiste.

Gerundives

1. Juratores dicunt super sacramentum suum quod predicta Alicia culpabilis est. Ideo suspendenda.

2. Quilibet liber homo de Risseby dat unum obulum pro aisamento pasture habendo.

3. Qui dicunt quod predictus Robert Kett de alta proditione et Guerra levanda versus dictum dominum regem indictatus fuit.

4. Habendum et tenedum predictum tenementum predicto Johanni.

Gerund Answers:

1. Likewise I bequeath to distribute among lepers of Norwich 40 pennies.

2. Peter of Nerford was attached to answer to Richard son of Turkil.

3. He holds a tenement by doing 12 plough-services per year.

4. I entrust my to body for burial in the church of Saint George.

5. By rendering thereafter annually to the aforesaid William and his assignees their one red rose for the birth feast of Saint John the Baptist.

Gerundive Answers:

1. The jurors declare their above-mentioned corporal oath whom the aforesaid Alice is guilty. Therefore, she is to be hanged.

2. Whichever free man of Risseby gives one half-penny in return for having easement of pasture.

3. Who say that the aforesaid Robert Kett was indicted of high treason and for raising war against the lord king.

4. To have and to hold the aforesaid tenement by the aforesaid John.

Subjunctive Verbs

We have spent a vast number of pages looking at the active and passive INDICATIVE verb. You will be pleased to know that each conjugation, active, passive, and tense has a subjunctive form.

The subjunctive is a **verbal mood**. It exists in most languages including English:

- *God **save** the Queen*
- *If I **were** you*
- *If the truth **be** told*

But the subjunctive is far more common in Latin. All the endings for each conjugation is given at the back of this book in the grammar sheets. You will note, however, that there is no future or future perfect subjunctive.

At this level of Latin, the subjunctive is rarely used – only in two main situations:

- Where something **MIGHT** happen
- Where something **OUGHT** to happen

Both can be translated as '*should*'. For example, '*If it should happen*' can also be translated as '*If it might happen.*'

A common use is in introductory phrases:

- *Sciant presentes et future quod* (Let those present and future know that...)

- *Noveritis quod* (Know that …)
- *Pateat universis per presentes* (Be it known to all men by these presents…)

- *Notum sit omnibus* (Let it be known to all men…)

The subjunctive can also be used after '*si*' (if) and '*ut*' (in order that):

- *Si contingat quod obierit sine herede.*
(If it happens that he dies without an heir…)

- *Faciendo xii aruras per annum si habeat carucam integram.*
(By performing 12 plough services a year if he has a whole ploughteam)

- *Ut hec carta mea rata sit et stabilis*
(In order that this my charter should be valid and settled)

'*Si*' (if) may also be followed by the **future perfect**, which looks almost the same as the perfect subjunctive. In practice there is little difference, but the perfect subjunctive is only used for an action in the past, whilst the future perfect refers to the future:

Charter Examples to Translate

Throughout this book we have looked at translating sentences and short paragraphs. Actual charters, however, can span a full page, or even longer. As a true testament to your newly acquired Medieval Latin skill, translate these following charters

Regarding the following charters, don't get overwhelmed by how long they are. All the words, tenses, and declensions within them have been covered in past chapters so use the grammar sheets and word lists at the back of this book to help you.

Remember too that there is no sentence order in latin, so it may help to translate the words as literal as possible first, then make the sentence grammatically correct after. As stated before, a good rule of thumb is to follow this formula:

Nominative Noun – Verb – Accusative Noun – Dative Noun

Everything in between this is just filler and legal jargon!

Good luck!

1. William Graindeorge grants to the monks, two bovates of land in Flasby fields with toft and croft and all other appurtenances, 1155-1190. (Taken from *The Coucher Book Of Furness Abbey, Book 8, p.360*)

As some background, a *Coucher Book* is a large book held by an abbey, monastery, or church that contains a collection of their legal documents such as charters. Often these are also known as *cartularies*.

Sciant omnes tam presentes quam futuri quod ego Willelmus Graindeorge de Flasceby concessu heredum meorum dedi et concessi et hac presenti carta mea confirmavi Deo et Deate Marie de Furnesio et monachis ibidem Deo servientibus pro salute anime mee et omnium antecessorum et successorum meorum in puram et perpetuam elemosinam duas bovatas terre in campis de Flasceby, illas scilicet que sunt propinquiores carcate terre Hugonis filii Willelmi ubique versus solem; cum tofto et crofto ad dictas bovatas pertinentibus, scilicet toftum et croftum que sunt inter toftum et croftum Radulfi fabri et croftum Johannis hominis Hugonis in Flasceby, cum omnibus pertentiis suis in bosco et plano, in pratis et pascuis, in viis et semitis, in moris et mariscis, in tubariis et in aquis et in omnibus libertatibus et aisiamentis et communibus eisdem ville ad prefatas bovatas terre pertinentibus infra villam et campos de Flasceby et extra.

Translation:

Know all men both present and future that I William Graindeorge of Flasby, with the assent of my heirs have given and granted and by this my present charter have confirmed to God and to Blessed Mary of Furness and to the monks serving God there for the salvation of my soul and of all my predecessors and successors in pure and perpetual alms two bovates of land in the fields of Flasby, namely those which are nearest to the carucate of land of Hugh son of William, on all sides facing the sun; with toft and croft pertaining to the said bovates, namely the toft and croft which are between the toft and croft of Ralph the smith and the croft of John, the man of Hugh in Flasby, with all their appurtenances in wood and plain, in meadows and pastures, in ways and paths, in moors and marshes, in turf-pits and in waters and in all liberties and easements and commons pertaining to the aforesaid bovates of land within the town and fields of Flasby and outside.

SECTION II

Miscellaneous Items

Charter Openings

The following are some of the very common charter openings with their respective translations:

- *Sciant Omnes Quod ...*
  – Know all men that.

- *Sciant presentes et futuri quod ...*
  – Know men present and future.

- *Noverint universi quod ...*
  – Know all that.

- *Noverint universi per presentes ...*
  – Know all men by these presents that

- *In Dei nominee, Amen.*
  – In the name of God, Amen.

- *Pateat per presentes quod...*
  – Be it known by these presents that

- *Universis Christi fidelibus pateat per presentes quod...*
  – To all Christ's faithful be it manifest by these presents that

Latin Names

As seen throughout this book, names in Latin have different endings. The following are some highly common medieval names with their Latin declensions.

1st Declension (Mainly Feminine)

Elizabeth	
Nom.	Elizabetha
Acc.	Elizabetham
Gen.	Elizabethe
Dat.	Elizabethe
Abl.	Elizabetha

Isabella	
Nom.	Isabella
Acc.	Isabellam
Gen.	Isabelle
Dat.	Isabelle
Abl.	Isabella

Mary	
Nom.	Maria
Acc.	Mariam
Gen.	Marie
Dat.	Marie
Abl.	Maria

Joan	
Nom.	Johanna
Acc.	Johannam
Gen.	Johanne
Dat.	Johanne
Abl.	Johanna

Thomas	
Nom.	Thomas
Acc.	Thomam
Gen.	Thome
Dat.	Thome
Abl.	Thoma

Adam	
Nom.	Adam
Acc.	Adam
Gen.	Ade
Dat.	Ade
Abl.	Ada

* Masculine names which are 1st Declension have irregular nominatives.

2nd Declension (Masculine)

Ralph	
Nom.	Radulphus
Acc.	Radulphum
Gen.	Radulphi
Dat.	Radulpho
Abl.	Radulpho

Henry	
Nom.	Henricus
Acc.	Henricum
Gen.	Henrici
Dat.	Henrico
Abl.	Henrico

James	
Nom.	Jacobus
Acc.	Jacobum
Gen.	Jacobi
Dat.	Jacobo
Abl.	Jacobo

Robert	
Nom.	Robertus
Acc.	Robertum
Gen.	Roberti
Dat.	Roberto
Abl.	Roberto

Roger	
Nom.	Rogerus
Acc.	Rogerum
Gen.	Rogeri
Dat.	Rogero
Abl.	Rogero

Richard	
Nom.	Ricardus
Acc.	Ricardum
Gen.	Richardi
Dat.	Richardo
Abl.	Richardo

Gilbert	
Nom.	Gilbertus
Acc.	Gilbertum
Gen.	Gilberti

Charles	
Nom.	Carolus
Acc.	Carolum
Gen.	Caroli

Dat.	Gilberto
Abl.	Gilberto

Dat.	Carolo
Abl.	Carolo

3rd Declension (Irregular with Stem Change)

John	
Nom.	Johannes
Acc.	Johannem
Gen.	Johannis
Dat.	Johanni
Abl.	Johanne

Hugo	
Nom.	Hugo
Acc.	Hugonem
Gen.	Hugonis
Dat.	Hugoni
Abl.	Hugone

Simon	
Nom.	Simo
Acc.	Simonem
Gen.	Simonis
Dat.	Simoni
Abl.	Simone

Michael	
Nom.	Michael
Acc.	Michaelem
Gen.	Michaelis
Dat.	Michaeli
Abl.	Michaele

Agnes	
Nom.	Agnes
Acc.	Agnetem
Gen.	Agnetis
Dat.	Agneti
Abl.	Agnete

Matilda	
Nom.	Mathildis
Acc.	Mathildem
Gen.	Mathildis
Dat.	Mathildi
Abl.	Mathilde

Numbers

The following are Latin numbers, there are two types known as **cardinal and ordinal**. Cardinal numbers are essentially *one, two, three*, whereas Ordinal numbers are *first, second, third*.

Numbers follow the same declension as 1st and 2nd declension adjectives. This means each number has variations in gender and case. Aside from 1, all numbers are obviously plural.

Its worth noting that Medieval Latin numerals will use a '*j*' instead of an '*i*' to show the end of a number sequence.

	Numeral	**Cardinal**	**Ordinal**
1	I / j	Unus, Una, Unum	Primus, -a,-um
2	ij	Duo, Due, Duo	Secundus/Alter
3	iij	Tres (m/f), Tria	Tercius
4	iiij / iv	Quattuor	Quartus
5	v	Quinque	Quintus
6	vj	Sex	Sextus
7	vij	Septem	Septimus
8	viij	Octo	Octavus
9	viiij / ix	Novem	Nonus
10	x	Decem	Decimus
11	xj	Undecim	Undecimus
12	xij	Duodecim	Duodecimus
13	xiij	Tredecim	Tercius Decimus
14-17		Cardinal Number + Decim	Ordinal Number + Decimus

18	xviij	Duodeviginti / Octodecim	Duedevicesimus / Octavus Decimus
	Numeral	**Cardinal**	**Ordinal**
19	xviiij / xix	Undeviginti / Novemdecim	Undevicesimus / Novnus Decimus
20	xx	Viginti	Vicesimus
21	xxj	Unus et Viginti / Viginti Unus	Unus et Vicesimus / Vicesimus Primus
22-29		Cardinal Number et Viginti	Ordinal Number et Vicesimus
All of the numbers from 20 onwards follow this formular of *'Cardinal/ Ordinal Number **et** Multiple of Ten'*			
30	xxx	Triginta	Tricesimus
40	xl	Quadraginta	Quadragesimus
50	L	Quinquaginta	Qinquagesimus
60	lx	Sexaginta	Sexagesimus
70	lxx	Septuaginta	Septuagesimus
80	lxxx / iiij^{xx}	Octoginta	Octogesimus
90	lxxxx / iiij^{xx}x	Nonaginta	Nonagesimus
100	c	Centum	Centesimus
200	cc	Ducenti / Ducente / Ducenta	Ducentesimus
300	ccc	Trecenti	Trecentesimus
400	cccc	Quadringenti	Quagringentesimus
500	d	Quingenti	Quingentesimus
600	dc	Sescenti	Sescentesimus
700	dcc	Septingenti	Septingentesimus

800	dccc	Octingenti	Octingentesimus
900	dcccc	Nongenti	Nongentesiumus
1000	m	Mille	Millesimus
2000	mm	Duo Milia	Bismillesimus

Grammar Sheets

Even after completing all the previous lessons, I hope that this book endures as a companion to beginner Latinists as the aim of this guide is to not only teach Medieval Latin to beginners, but to enable you to tackle contemporary sources and translate material using the following sections I have assembled.

As such, I have compiled all of the following:

- Noun Declensions
- Adjective Declensions
- Pronoun and Prenominal Adjective Declensions
- Personal Pronoun Declensions
- Comparative Adjective and Adverb Declension
- Verb Conjugations

All of which are within this book but are now in one place to allow you to translate quickly and easily.

DECLENSION OF NOUNS

1ˢᵗ Declension – Feminine

Terra – Land

FEMININE	Singular	Plural	
Nominative	Terra	Terre	*Subject*
Accusative	Terram	Terras	*Object*
Genitive	Terre	Terrarum	*Of*
Dative	Terre	Terris	*To/For*
Ablative	Terra	Terris	*By/With/From*

2ⁿᵈ Declension – Masculine or Neuter

Dominus – Lord

MASCULINE	Singular	Plural
Nominative	Dominus	Domini
Accusative	Dominum	Dominos
Genitive	Domini	Dominorum
Dative	Domino	Dominis
Ablative	Domino	Dominis

Messuagium – Messuage

NEUTER	Singular	Plural
Nominative	Messuagium	Messuagia
Accusative	Messuagium	Messuagia
Genitive	Messuagii	Messuagiorum
Dative	Messuagio	Messuagiis
Ablative	Messuagio	Messuagiis

3<u>rd</u> Declension – Masculine, Feminine, or Neuter

Rex, Regis – King

MASCULINE	Singular	Plural
Nominative	Rex	Reges
Accusative	Regem	Reges
Genitive	Regis	Regum
Dative	Regi	Regibus
Ablative	Rege	Regibus

* Masculine and Feminine nouns have the same ending

Nomen, Nominis – Name

NEUTER	Singular	Plural
Nominative	Nomen	Nomina
Accusative	Nomen	Nomina
Genitive	Nominis	Nominum
Dative	Nomini	Nominibus
Ablative	Nomine	Nominibus

4th Declension – Masculine, Feminine, or Neuter

* Neuters, however, are rare in medieval documents

MASCULINE	Singular	Plural
Nominative	Obitus	Obitus
Accusative	Obitum	Obitus
Genitive	Obitus	Obituum
Dative	Obitui	Obitibus
Ablative	Obitu	Obitibus

DECLENSION OF ADJECTIVES

1st and 2nd Declension

Predictus – Aforesaid

	SINGULAR		
	Masculine	**Feminine**	**Neuter**
Nom.	Predictus	Predicta	Predictum
Acc.	Predictum	Predictam	Predictum
Gen.	Predicti	Predicte	Predicti
Dat.	Predicto	Predicte	Predicto
Abl.	Predicto	Predicta	Predicto

	PLURAL		
	Masculine	**Feminine**	**Neuter**
Nom.	Predicti	Predicte	Predicta
Acc.	Predictos	Predictas	Predicta
Gen.	Predictorum	Predictarum	Predictorum
Dat.	Predictis		
Abl.			

3nd Declension

(Part 1) *Omnis, Omne* – All/Whole

	SINGULAR		
	Masculine	**Feminine**	**Neuter**
Nom.	*Omnis*	*Omnis*	*Omne*
Acc.	*Omnem*	*Omnem*	*Omne*
Gen.	*Omnis*		
Dat.	*Omni*		
Abl.			

	PLURAL		
	Masculine	**Feminine**	**Neuter**
Nom.	Omnes	Omnes	Omnia
Acc.	Omnes	Omnes	Omnia
Gen.	Omnium		
Dat.	Omnibus		
Abl.			

(Part 2) *Ingens, Ingentis* – Huge

	SINGULAR		
	Masculine	**Feminine**	**Neuter**
Nom.	Ingens	Ingens	Ingens
Acc.	Ingentem	Ingentem	Ingens
Gen.	Ingentis		
Dat.	Ingenti		
Abl.			

	PLURAL		
	Masculine	Feminine	Neuter
Nom.	Ingentes	Ingentes	Ingentia
Acc.	Ingentes	Ingentes	Ingentia
Gen.	Ingentium		
Dat.	Ingentibus		
Abl.			

DECLENSION OF PRONOUNS AND PRENOMINAL ADJECTIVES

Allius, Alia, Aliud – Other

Singular	Masculine	Feminine	Neuter
Nom.	Alius	Alia	Aliud
Acc.	Alium	Aliam	Aliud
Gen.	Alius	Alius	Alius
Dat.	Alii	Alii	Alii
Abl.	Alio	Alio	Alio

Plural	Masculine	Feminine	Neuter
Nom.	Alii	Alie	Alia
Acc.	Alios	Alias	Alia
Gen.	Aliorum	Aliarum	Aliorum
Dat.	Aliis	Aliis	Aliis
Abl.	Aliis	Aliis	Aliis

Idem, Eadem, Idem – The Same

Singular	Masculine	Feminine	Neuter
Nom.	Idem	Eadem	Idem
Acc.	Eundem	Eandem	Idem
Gen.	Euisdem	Euisdem	Euisdem
Dat.	Eidem	Eidem	Eidem
Abl.	Eodem	Eadem	Eodem

Plural	Masculine	Feminine	Neuter
Nom.	Eidem	Eedem	eadem
Acc.	Eosdem	Easdem	Eadem
Gen.	Eorundem	Earundem	Eurundem
Dat.	Eisdem	Eisdem	Eisdem

Abl.	Eisdem	Eisdem	Eisdem

Ille, Illa, Illud – That, Those

Singular	Masculine	Feminine	Neuter
Nom.	Ille	Illa	Illud
Acc.	Illum	Illam	Illud
Gen.	Illius	Illius	Illius
Dat.	Illi	Illi	Illi
Abl.	Illo	Illa	Illo

Plural	Masculine	Feminine	Neuter
Nom.	Illi	Ille	Illa
Acc.	Illos	Illas	Illa
Gen.	Illorum	Illarum	Illorum
Dat.	Illis	Illis	Illis
Abl.	Illis	Illis	Illis

Ipse, Ipsa, Ipsum – Self

Singular	Masculine	Feminine	Neuter
Nom.	Ipse	Ipsa	Ipsum
Acc.	Ipsum	Ipsam	Ipsum
Gen.	Ipsius	Ipsius	Ipsius
Dat.	Ipsi	Ipsi	Ipsi
Abl.	Ipso	Ipsa	Ipso

Plural	Masculine	Feminine	Neuter
Nom.	Ipsi	Ipse	Ipsa
Acc.	Ipsos	Ipsas	Ipsa
Gen.	Ipsorum	Ipsarum	Ipsorum
Dat.	Ipsis	Ipsis	Ipsis
Abl.	Ipsis	Ipsis	Ipsis

Quidam, Quedam, Quoddam – A Certain

Singular	Masculine	Feminine	Neuter
Nom.	Quidam	Quedam	Quoddam
Acc.	Quendam	Quandam	Quoddam
Gen.	Cuiusdam	Cuiusdam	Cuiusdam
Dat.	Cuidam	Cuidam	Cuidam
Abl.	Quodam	Quodam	Quodam

Plural	Masculine	Feminine	Neuter
Nom.	Quidam	Quedam	Quedam
Acc.	Quosdam	Quasdam	Quedam
Gen.	Quorundam	Quarundam	Quorundam
Dat.	Quibusdam		
Abl.			

Quilibet – Any, Each, Whatsoever, Whoever

Singular	Masculine	Feminine	Neuter
Nom.	Quilibet	Quelibet	Quodlibet
Acc.	Quenlibet	Quanlibet	Quodlibet
Gen.	Cuiuslibet	Cuiuslibet	Cuiuslibet
Dat.	Cuilibet	Cuilibet	Cuilibet
Abl.	Quolibet	Quolibet	Quolibet

Plural	Masculine	Feminine	Neuter
Nom.	Quilibet	Quelibet	Quelibet
Acc.	Quoslibet	Quaslibet	Quelibet
Gen.	Quorunlibet	Quarunlibet	Quorunlibet
Dat.	Quibuslibet		
Abl.			

Qui, Que, Quod – Who, Whom, Which, That

Singular	Masculine	Feminine	Neuter
Nom.	Qui	Que	Quod
Acc.	Quem	Quam	Quod
Gen.	Cuius	Cuius	Cuius
Dat.	Cui	Cui	Cui
Abl.	Quo	Qua	Quo

Plural	Masculine	Feminine	Neuter
Nom.	Qui	Que	Que
Acc.	Quos	Quas	Que
Gen.	Quorum	Quarum	Quorum
Dat.	Quibus		
Abl.			

Hic, Hec, Hoc – This, That

Singular	Masculine	Feminine	Neuter
Nom.	Hic	Hec	Hoc
Acc.	Hunc	Hanc	Hoc
Gen.	Huius	Huius	Huius
Dat.	Huic	Huic	Huic
Abl.	Hoc	Hac	Hoc

Plural	Masculine	Feminine	Neuter
Nom.	Hi	He	Hec
Acc.	Hos	Has	Hec
Gen.	Horum	Horum	Horum
Dat.	Hiis	Hiis	Hiis
Abl.	Hiis	Hiis	Hiis

DECLENSION OF PERSONAL PRONOUNS

Ego – I

	I	You (s)	He/She/ It/They	We	You (pl)
Nom.	Ego	Tu		Nos	Vos
Acc.	Me	Te	Se	Nos	Vos
Gen.	Mei	Tui	Sui	Nostri/ Nostrum	Vesti/ Vestrum
Dat.	Mihi	Tibi	Sibi	Nobis	Vobis
Abl.	Me	Te	Se	Nobis	Vobis

Meus – My

Singular	Masc.	Fem.	Neuter
Nom.	Meus	Mea	Meum
Acc.	Meum	Meam	Meum
Gen.	Mei	Mee	Mei
Dat.	Meo	Mee	Meo
Abl.	Meo	Mea	Meo

Suus – His/Her/Their

Singular	Masc.	Fem.	Neuter
Nom.	Suus	Sua	Suum
Acc.	Suum	Suam	Suum
Gen.	Sui	Sue	Sui
Dat.	Suo	Sue	Suo
Abl.	Suo	Sua	Suo

Euis – He/She/It/They/Her/His/Their

Singular	Masc.	Fem.	Neuter
Nom.	Is	Ea	Id
Acc.	Eum	Eam	Id
Gen.	Euis	Euis	Euis
Dat.	Ei	Ei	Ei
Abl.	Eo	Ea	Eo

DECLENSION OF COMPARATIVE ADJECTIVES AND ADVERBS

Comparative Declension:

Latus – Wide

Singular	Masculine	Feminine	Neuter
Nom.	Latior	Latior	Latius
Acc.	Latiorem	Latiorem	Latius
Gen.	Latioris	Latioris	Latioris
Dat.	Latiori	Latiori	Latiori
Abl.	Latiore	Latiore	Latiore

Plural	Masculine	Feminine	Neuter
Nom.	Latiores	Latiores	Latiora
Acc.	Latiores	Latiores	Latiora
Gen.	Latiorum		
Dat.	Latioribus		
Abl.			

Adverb Declension:

	Comparative	Superlative
Breviter – Briefly	Brevius	Brevissime
Facile – Easily	Facilius	Facillime

Adverbs generally end in either *-e* or *-ter* and do not decline.

Present	Group 1	Group 2
I	Confirmav–**i**	Tenu–**i**
You (s)	Confirmav–**isti**	Tenu–**isti**
He/She/It	Confirmav–**it**	Tenu–**it**
We	Confirmav–**imus**	Tenu–**imus**
You (pl)	Confirmav–**istis**	Tenu–**istis**
They	Confirmav–**erunt**	Tenu–**erunt**

Present	Group 3	Group 4
I	Concess–**i**	Serviv–**i**
You (s)	Concess–**isti**	Serviv–**isti**
He/She/It	Concess–**it**	Serviv–**it**
We	Concess–**imus**	Serviv–**imus**
You (pl)	Concess–**istis**	Serviv–**istis**
They	Concess–**erunt**	Serviv–**erunt**

Present	Group 1	Group 2
I	Confirm–**o**	Ten–**eo**
You (s)	Confirm–**as**	Ten–**es**
He/She/It	Confirm–**at**	Ten–**et**
We	Confirm–**amus**	Ten–**emus**
You (pl)	Confirm–**atis**	Ten–**etis**
They	Confirm–**ant**	Ten–**ent**

Present	Group 3	Group 4
I	Conced–**o**	Serv–**io**
You (s)	Conced–**is**	Serv–**is**
He/She/It	Conced–**it**	Serv–**it**
We	Conced–**imus**	Serv–**imus**
You (pl)	Conced–**I**	Serv–**I**

| They | Conced–**unt** | Serv–**iunt** |

DECLENSION OF VERBS

1st Conjugation –

Confirmo, Confirmare, Confirmavi, Confirmatum – To Confirm

ACTIVE Indicative		
Present – I Confirm	**Imperfect – I used to Confirm**	**Future – I will Confirm**
Confirm**o** *(I)*	Confirma**bam**	Confirma**bo**
Confirm**as** *(You s.)*	Confirma**bas**	Confirma**bis**
Confirm**at** *(He/She/It)*	Confirma**bat**	Confirma**bit**
Confirm**amus** *(We)*	Confirma**bamus**	Confirma**bimus**
Confirm**atis** *(You pl.)*	Confirma**batis**	Confirma**bitis**
Confirm**ant** *(They)*	Confirma**bant**	Confirma**bunt**
Perfect – I Confirmed	**Future Perfect – I shall have Confirmed**	**Pluperfect – I had Called**
Confirma**vi**	Confirma**vero**	Confirma**veram**
Confirma**visti**	Confirma**veris**	Confirma**veras**
Confirma**vit**	Confirma**verit**	Confirma**verat**
Confirma**vimus**	Confirma**verimus**	Confirma**veramus**
Confirma**vistis**	Confirma**veristis**	Confirma**veratis**
Confirma**verunt**	Confirma**verint**	Confirma**verant**

144

ACTIVE Subjunctive	
Present – I Confirm	**Imperfect – I used to Confirm**
Confirmem *(I)*	*Confirmarem*
Confirmes *(You s.)*	*Confirmares*
Confirmet *(He/She/It)*	*Confirmaret*
Confirmemus *(We)*	*Confirmaremus*
Confirmetis *(You pl.)*	*Confirmaretis*
Confirment *(They)*	*Confirmarent*
Perfect – I Confirmed	**Pluperfect – I had Called**
Confirmaverim	*Confirmavissem*
Confirmaveris	*Confirmavisses*
Confirmaverit	*Confirmavisset*
Confirmaverimus	*Confirmavissemus*
Confirmaveritis	*Confirmavissetis*
Confirmaverint	*Confirmavissent*

Other Forms	
Gerund	*Confirmandum, -i*
Gerundives	*Confirmandus, -a, -um*

Supine	Confirmatum, -a, -um
Infinitive (*Present, Perfect*)	Confirmare, Confirmavisse

1st Conjugation –

Confirmo, -are, -avi, -atum – To Confirm

PASSIVE Indicative		
Present – **I Confirm**	**Imperfect –** **I used to be** **Confirmed**	**Future –** **I will be** **Confirmed**
*Confirm**or** (I)*	*Confirma**bar***	*Confirma**bor***
*Confirm**aris** (You s.)*	*Confirma**baris***	*Confirma**beris***
*Confirm**atur** (He/She/It)*	*Confirma**batur***	*Confirma**bitur***
*Confirm**amur** (We)*	*Confirma**bamur***	*Confirma**bimur***
*Confirm**amini** (You pl.)*	*Confirma**bamini***	*Confirma**bimini***
*Confirm**antur** (They)*	*Confirma**bantur***	*Confirma**buntur***
Perfect – I was **Confirmed**	**Future Perfect – I** **shall have been** **Confirmed**	**Pluperfect – I** **had been Called**
*Confirm**atus, a, um** **fui***	*Confirm**atus** **fuero***	*Confirm**atus** **fueram***
*Confirm**atus fuisti***	*Confirm**atus** **fueris***	*Confirm**atus** **fueras***
*Confirm**atus fuit***	*Confirm**atus** **fuerit***	*Confirm**atus** **fuerat***
*Confirm**ati, e, a** **fuimus***	*Confirm**ati** **fuerimus***	*Confirm**ati** **fueramus***
*Confirm**ati fuistis***	*Confirm**ati** **fueritis***	*Confirm**ati** **fueratis***

147

Confirmati fuerunt	Confirmati fuerint	Confirmati fuerant

PASSIVE Subjunctive

Present – I Confirm	Imperfect – I used to be Confirmed
Confirmor	Confirmarer
Confirmeris	Confirmareris
Confirmetur	Confirmaretur
Confirmemur	Confirmaremur
Confirmemini	Confirmaremini
Confirmentur	Confirmarentur
Perfect – I was Confirmed	**Pluperfect – I had been Called**
Confirmatus fuerim	Confirmatus fuissem
Confirmatus fueris	Confirmatus fuisses
Confirmatus fuerit	Confirmatus fuisset
Confirmati fuerimus	Confirmati fuissemus
Confirmati fueristis	Confirmati fuisetis
Confirmati fuerint	Confirmati fuissent

Alternative Present (Indicative) Form
Confirmatus, (-a, -um) **sum**
Confirmatus **es**
Confirmatus **est**

148

Confirm**ati** (-e, -a) **sumus**
Confirm**ati estis**
Confirm**ati sunt**

2nd Conjugation –

Teneo, Tenere, Tenui, Tenitum – To Hold

ACTIVE Indicative		
Present – I Hold	**Imperfect – I used to Hold**	**Future – I will Hold**
Teneo (I)	*Tenebam*	*Tenebo*
Tenes (You s.)	*Tenebas*	*Tenebis*
Tenet (He/She/It)	*Tenebat*	*Tenebit*
Tenemus (We)	*Tenebamus*	*Tenebimus*
Tenetis (You pl.)	*Tenebatis*	*Tenebitis*
Tenent (They)	*Tenebant*	*Tenebunt*
Perfect – I Held	**Future Perfect – I shall have Held**	**Pluperfect – I had Held**
Tenui	*Tenuero*	*Tenueram*
Tenuisti	*Tenueris*	*Tenueras*
Tenuit	*Tenuerit*	*Tenuerat*
Tenuimus	*Tenuerimus*	*Tenueramus*
Tenuistis	*Tenueristis*	*Tenueratis*
Tenuerunt	*Tenuerint*	*Tenuerant*

ACTIVE Subjunctive	
Present – I Held	**Imperfect – I used to Hold**
Teneam *(I)*	*Tenerem*
Teneas *(You s.)*	*Teneres*
Teneat *(He/She/It)*	*Teneret*
Teneamus *(We)*	*Teneremus*
Teneatis *(You pl.)*	*Teneretis*
Teneant *(They)*	*Tenerent*
Perfect – I Held	**Pluperfect – I had Held**
Tenuerim	*Tenuissem*
Tenueris	*Tenuisses*
Tenuerit	*Tenuisset*
Tenuerimus	*Tenuissemus*
Tenueritis	*Tenuissetis*
Tenuerint	*Tenuissent*

Other Forms	
Gerund	*Tenendum, -i*
Gerundives	*Tenendus, -a, -um*

Supine	*Tenitum, -a, -um*
Infinitive (*Present, Perfect*)	*Tenere, Tenuisse*

2nd Conjugation –

Teneo, -ere, -ui, -itum – To Hold

PASSIVE Indicative		
Present – I Hold	Imperfect – I used to be Held	Future – I will be Held
Teneor (I)	*Tenebar*	*Tenebor*
Teneris *(You s.)*	*Tenebaris*	*Teneberis*
Tenetur (He/She/It)	*Tenebatur*	*Tenebitur*
Tenemur *(We)*	*Tenebamur*	*Tenebimur*
Tenemini *(You pl.)*	*Tenebamini*	*Tenebimini*
Tenentur *(They)*	*Tenebantur*	*Tenebuntur*
Perfect – I was Held	Future Perfect – I shall have been Held	Pluperfect – I had been Held
Tenitus, a, um fui	*Tenitus fuero*	*Tenitus fueram*
Tenitus fuisti	*Tenitus fueris*	*Tenitus fueras*
Tenitus fuit	*Tenitus fuerit*	*Tenitus fuerat*
Teniti, e, a fuimus	*Teniti fuerimus*	*Tenitus* *fueramus*
Teniti fuistis	*Teniti fueritis*	*Tenitus fueratis*
Teniti fuerunt	*Teniti fuerint*	*Tenitus fuerant*

PASSIVE Subjunctive	
Present – I Hold	**Imperfect – I used to be Held**
Tenear	*Tenerer*
Tenearis	*Tenereris*
Teneatur	*Teneretur*
Teneamur	*Teneremur*
Teneamini	*Teneremini*
Teneantur	*Tenerentur*
Perfect – I was Held	**Pluperfect – I had been Held**
Tenitus fuerim	*Tenitus fuissem*
Tenitus fueris	*Tenitus fuisses*
Tenitus fuerit	*Tenitus fuisset*
Teniti fuerimus	*Teniti fuissemus*
Teniti fueristis	*Teniti fuisetis*
Teniti fuerint	*Teniti fuissent*

Alternative Present (Indicative) Form
Teni**tus**, (-a, -um) **sum**
Teni**tus es**
Teni**tus est**
Teniti (-e, -a) **sumus**
Teniti **estis**
Teniti **sunt**

3rd Conjugation –

Concedo, Concedere, Concessi, Concessum – To Grant

ACTIVE Indicative		
Present – I Grant	**Imperfect – I used to Grant**	**Future – I will Grant**
Concedo (I)	*Concedebam*	*Concedam*
Concedis (You s.)	*Concedebas*	*Concedes*
Concedit (He/She/It)	*Concedebat*	*Concedet*
Concedimus (We)	*Concedebamus*	*Concedemus*
Conceditis (You pl.)	*Concedebatis*	*Concedetis*
Concedunt (They)	*Concedebant*	*Concedent*
Perfect – I Granted	**Future Perfect – I shall have Granted**	**Pluperfect – I had Granted**
Concessi	*Concessero*	*Concesseram*
Concessisti	*Concesseris*	*Concesseras*
Concessit	*Concesserit*	*Concesserat*
Concessimus	*Concesserimus*	*Concesseramus*
Concessistis	*Concesseristis*	*Concesseratis*
Concesserunt	*Concesserint*	*Concesserant*

ACTIVE Subjunctive	
Present – I Granted	**Imperfect – I used to Grant**
Conced*am* (I)	Conced*erem*
Conced*as* (You s.)	Conced*eres*
Conced*at* (He/She/It)	Conced*eret*
Conced*amus* (We)	Conced*eremus*
Conced*atis* (You pl.)	Conced*eretis*
Conced*ant* (They)	Conced*erent*
Perfect – I Granted	**Pluperfect – I had Granted**
Concess*erim*	Concess*issem*
Concess*eris*	Concess*isses*
Concess*erit*	Concess*isset*
Concess*erimus*	Concess*issemus*
Concess*eritis*	Concess*issetis*
Concess*erint*	Concess*issent*

Other Forms	
Gerund	Concendum, -i
Gerundives	Concendus, -a, -um
Supine	Concessum
Infinitive (*Present, Perfect*)	Concedere, Concessisse

3rd Conjugation –

Concedo, -dere, -cessi, -cessum – To Grant

PASSIVE Indicative		
Present – I Grant	**Imperfect – I used to be Granted**	**Future – I will be Granted**
Concedor (I)	*Concedebar*	*Concedar*
Concederis (You s.)	*Concedebaris*	*Concederis*
Conceditur (He/She/It)	*Concedebatur*	*Concedetur*
Concedimur (We)	*Concedebamur*	*Concedemur*
Concedimini (You pl.)	*Concedebamini*	*Concedemini*
Conceduntur (They)	*Concedebantur*	*Concedentur*
Perfect – I was Granted	**Future Perfect – I shall have been Granted**	**Pluperfect – I had been Granted**
Concessus, a, um fui	*Concessus fuero*	*Concessus fueram*
Concessus fuisti	*Concessus fueris*	*Concessus fueras*
Concessus fuit	*Concessus fuerit*	*Concessus fuerat*
Concessi, e, a fuimus	*Concessi fuerimus*	*Concessi fueramus*
Concessi fuistis	*Concessi fueritis*	*Concessi fueratis*
Concessi fuerunt	*Concessi fuerint*	*Concessi fuerant*

PASSIVE Subjunctive	
Present – I Grant	**Imperfect – I used to be Granted**
Concedar	*Concederer*
Concedaris	*Concedereris*
Concedatur	*Concederetur*
Concedamur	*Concederemur*
Concedamini	*Concederemini*
Concedantur	*Concederentur*
Perfect – I was Granted	**Pluperfect – I had been Granted**
Concessus fuerim	*Concessus fuissem*
Concessus fueris	*Concessus fuisses*
Concessus fuerit	*Concessus fuisset*
Concessi fuerimus	*Concessi fuissemus*
Concessi fueristis	*Concessi fuisetis*
Concessi fuerint	*Concessi fuissent*

Alternative Present (Indicative) Form
Concessus, (-a, -um) **sum**
Concessus **es**
Concessus **est**
Concessi (-e, -a) **sumus**
Concessi **estis**
Concessi **sunt**

4rd Conjugation –

Servio, Servire, Servivi, Servitum – To Serve

ACTIVE Indicative		
Present – I Hold	**Imperfect – I used to Hold**	**Future – I will Hold**
Servio (I)	*Serviebam*	*Serviam*
Servis (You s.)	*Serviebas*	*Servies*
Servit (He/She/It)	*Serviebat*	*Serviet*
Servimus (We)	*Serviebamus*	*Serviemus*
Servitis (You pl.)	*Serviebatis*	*Servietis*
Serviunt (They)	*Serviebant*	*Servient*
Perfect – I Held	**Future Perfect – I shall have Held**	**Pluperfect – I had Held**
Servivi	*Servivero*	*Serviveram*
Servivisti	*Serviveris*	*Serviveras*
Servivit	*Serviverit*	*Serviverat*
Servivimus	*Serviverimus*	*Serviveramus*
Servivistis	*Serviveritis*	*Serviveratis*
Serviverunt	*Serviverint*	*Serviverant*

ACTIVE Subjunctive	
Present – I Held	**Imperfect – I used to Hold**
Serviam *(I)*	*Servirem*
Servias *(You s.)*	*Servires*
Serviat *(He/She/It)*	*Serviret*
Serviamus *(We)*	*Serviremus*
Serviatis *(You pl.)*	*Serviretis*
Serviant *(They)*	*Servirent*
Perfect – I Held	**Pluperfect – I had Held**
Serviverim	*Servivissem*
Serviveris	*Servivisses*
Serviverit	*Servivisset*
Serviverimus	*Servivissemus*
Serviveristis	*Servivissetis*
Serviverint	*Servivissent*

Other Forms	
Gerund	*Serviendum, -i*
Gerundives	*Serviendus, -a, -um*
Supine	*Servitum*
Infinitive (*Present, Perfect*)	*Servire, Servivisse*

160

4th Conjugation –

Servio, -ire, -vi, -itum – To Serve

PASSIVE Indicative		
Present – I Hold	**Imperfect –** **I used to be Held**	**Future –** **I will be Held**
Servior (I)	*Serviebar*	*Serviar*
Serviris *(You s.)*	*Serviebaris*	*Servieris*
Servitur (He/She/It)	*Serviebatur*	*Servietur*
Servimur *(We)*	*Serviebamur*	*Serviemur*
Servimini *(You pl.)*	*Serviebamini*	*Serviemini*
Serviuntur *(They)*	*Serviebantur*	*Servientur*
Perfect – I was Held	**Future Perfect – I shall have been Held**	**Pluperfect – I had been Held**
Servitus, a, um fui	*Servitus fuero*	*Servitus fueram*
Servitus fuisti	*Servitus fueris*	*Servitus fueras*
Servitus fuit	*Servitus fuerit*	*Servitus fuerat*
Serviti, e, a fuimus	*Serviti fuerimus*	*Serviti fueramus*
Serviti fuistis	*Serviti fueritis*	*Serviti fueratis*
Serviti fuerunt	*Serviti fuerint*	*Serviti fuerant*

PASSIVE Subjunctive	
Present – I Hold	**Imperfect – I used to be Held**
Serviar	*Servirer*
Serviaris	*Servireris*
Serviatur	*Serviretur*
Serviamur	*Serviremur*
Serviamini	*Serviremini*
Serviantur	*Servirentur*
Perfect – I was Held	**Pluperfect – I had been Held**
Servitus fuerim	*Servitus fuissem*
Servitus fueris	*Servitus fuisses*
Servitus fuerit	*Servitus fuisset*
Serviti fuerimus	*Serviti fuissemus*
Serviti fueristis	*Serviti fuisetis*
Serviti fuerint	*Serviti fuissent*

Alternative Present (Indicative) Form
Servitus, (-a, -um) **sum**
Servitus **es**
Servitus **est**
Serviti (-e, -a) **sumus**
Serviti **estis**
Serviti **sunt**

WORD LIST

This word list is an attempt to gather, in one place, as much vocabulary needed to translate most medieval documents. Whilst it is not a dictionary that will give word definitions, it aims to provide a direct Latin-to-English translation so that if you do come across an unfamiliar word, you can look it up here in here and find its English equivalent.

The key aspects to know about this word list are listed below:

Nouns are given in the nominative form followed by the genitive ending, gender, and english translation.

> *Abbatia, -ie (f.) – Abbey*

Verbs are given in the first-person present form followed by their conjugation number. For 3rd Conjugation irregular verbs, the 1st Person Present, Infinitive, 1st Person Perfect, and Supine is given.

> *Lego (1) – To Bequeath*

> *Condo, -ere, -didi, -ditum (3) – To Construct*

Adjectives, like nouns, are also given in the nominative with a genitive ending and English translation but it will also note the different gendered endings to distinguish its declensions.

> Bonus, -a, -um (adj.) – Good

Omnis, -e (adj.) – All, Whole

Note that there is flexibility in the use of i and j. For example: Jaceo/iaceo, ius/jus, peius/pejus. If you can't find the word in one section, then try the other. The letters u and v are also interchangeable but that should not matter too much as usually these are within a word rather than the beginning letter.

Ultimately, the joy of Medieval Latin is that it is a puzzle. Unlike modern foreign languages at school where you must speak, memorise, listen, read, and write – Medieval Latin is purely translation. As such, there is no shame in using this word list to translate every word in a text. What you will find too is that over time you will be familiar with the more common Latin words and be quicker at finding new ones in the list.

Use this word list as a tool for successful and effective translation for this guide and further Latin study.

A, ab, abs – From, by

Abbas, Abbatis (m.) – Abbot

Abbatia, -ie (f.) – Abbey

Abduco, -ere, -duxi, -ductum (3) – To lead away

Absolute (adv.) – Entirely

Abutto (1) – To border upon

Ac, Atque – And

Accipio, -ere, -cepi, -ceptum (3) – To receive

Accommodo (1) – To accommodate, To lend

Acra, -e (f.) – An Acre

Ad – Towards, To, At, For

Ad Festum – At the feast

Adhuc (adv.) – Thus far, Hitherto

Adiacens, -entis (adj.) – Adjacent to

Admitto, -ere, -missi, -missum (3) – To Admit, Acknowledge

Adventus, -us (m.) – Advent, Arrival

Advocatus, -i (m.) – Patron

Affido (1) – Declare on oath

Agnus, -i (m.) – A Lamb

Ago, -ere, egi, actum (3) – To act

Agricola, -e (f.) – Husbandman

Alius, Alia, Aliud (pronoun) – Other

Allego (1) – To Allege

Altare, -is (n.) – An Altar

Alter, Altera, Alterum (adj.) – The Other

Altus, -a, -um (adj.) – High

Annuatim (adv.) – Annually

Annus, -i (m.) – Year

Annuus, -a, -um (adj.) – Annual

Ante – Before

Ante Manum – Beforehand

Antecessor, -oris (m.) – Ancestor (m.)

Antecessatrix, -icis (f.) – Ancestor (f.)

Antedictus, -a, -um (adj.) – Aforesaid

Apparentia, -ie (f.) – Appearance in Court

Appendicium, -ii (n.) – Appurtenance

Apud – At, By, Near, To, Towards

Aqua, -e (f.) – Water

Arabilis, -e (adj.) – Arable

Aratrum, -i (n.) – A plough of land

Assalto (1) – To Assault

Assensus, -us (m.) – Agreement

Assignatus, -i (m.) – An Assign

Assigno (1) – To Appoint

Attornatus, -i (m.) – Attorney

Audio, -ire, -ivi, -itum (4) – To Hear

Aufero, Auferre, Abstuli, Ablatum (3) – To Carry Away

Aula Regis – King's Court

Australis, -e (adj.) – Southern

Bonus, -a, -um (adj.) – Good

Borialis, -e (adj.) – Northern

Bovata, -e (f.) – A Bovate

Brevis, Breve (adj.) – Short

Burgus, -i (m.) – A town, Borough

Calumnio (1) – To Challenge

Campus, -i _m.) – A field

Canis, -is – Dog

Capellanus, -i (m.) – A chaplain

Capio, -ere, cepi, captum (3) – To Take

Carruca, -e (f.) – Plough, Carucate

Carta, -e (f.) – Charter

Cathedralis, -e (adj.) – Of, or For a cathedral

Celebro (1) – To celebrate Mass

Civis, -is (m.) – Citizen

Civitas, -tatis (f.) – A City, Capital

Clamo (1) – To Claim

Clamare Quietum – To quitclaim

Clericus, -i (m.) – Clerk

Clericus Parochialis – Parish Clerk

Cognosco, -ere, -gnovi, cognitum (3) – To Know

Concedo, -ere, -cessi, -cessum (3) – To Grant

Condo, -ere, -didi, -ditum (3) – To Construct

Condo Testamentum – To make a will

Confero, -ferre, -tuli, -latum (3) – To Confer

Conficio, -ere, -feci,-fectum (3) – To Confect

Confirmo (1) – To Confirm

Conquestus, -us (m.) – the Conquest (1066)

Consentio, -ire, -sensi, -sensum (4) – To Agree

Constituto, -ere, -stitui, -stitutum (3) – To Esbalish

Consuetudo Anglie – Common Law

Consuetudo Regni – Common Law

Corporalis, -e (adj.) – Physical

Corpus, -corporis (m.) – Body

Credo, -ere, -didi, -ditum (3) – To Believe

Crofta, -e (f.) – Croft

Croftum, -i (n.) – Croft

Cum – With

Curia, -e (f.) – Court of Law, King's Court

Data, Datum, Datus – Date

Datus (past part.) – Given

De – From, Of

Debeo (2) – I owe

Debitum, -i (n) – Debt

Defalta, -e (f.) – Defection

Deus, -i (m.) – God

Demonstro (1) – To Show

Dico, -ere, dixi, dictum (3) – To Say

Dictus, -a, -um (adj.) – Aforesaid

Dies – Day

Dies Dominica – Sunday

Dies Iovis – Thursday

Dies Lune – Monday

Dies Martis – Tuesday

Dies Mercurii – Wednesday

Dies Sabbati – Saturday

Dies Veneris – Friday

Dies Veneris Sanctus – Good Friday

Dies Veneris Parasceves – Good Friday

Difficilis, -e (adj.) – Difficult

Dimidia, -e (f.) – Half

Dimidius, -a, -um (adj.) – Half

Diocesis, -is (f.) – Diocese

Distribuo (3) – To Distribute, Divide

Distringo, -ere, -nxi, -ctum (3) – To Distrain

Do, Dare, Dedi, Datum (1) – To Give

Domina, -e (f.) – Lady

Dominus, -i (m.) – Lord

Domus, -us (f.) – House

Donum, -i (n.) – Gift

Duco, -ere, duxi, ductum (3) – To Lead

Edifico (1) – To Build

Ego – I

Eo, ire, ivi, itum (4) – To Go

Episcopalis, -e (adj) – Episcopal

Episcopus, -i (m.) – Bishop

Esse – To Be

Et – And

Facilis, -e (adj.) – Easy

Facio, -ere, feci, factum (3) – To Do

Femina – Wife, Woman

Feodum, -i (n.) – Fief, Fee

Festum, -i (n.) – Feast, Festival

Fidelitas, -atis (f.) – Fealty

Fides, Fidei (f.) – Faith

Filius, -ii (m.) – Son

Filia, (f.) – Daughter

Fossa, -e (f.) – Embankment

Frater, Fratris (m.) – Monk, Brother

Furo (1) – To Steal

Futurus, -a, -um (adj.) – Future

Gardianus, -i (m.) – Churchwarden

Grossus, -a, -um (adj.) – Thick

Habeo, -ere, Habui, Habitum (2) – To Have

Hereditaria, -e (f.) – Heiress

Hereditarie (adv.) – By inheritance

Hereditarius, -a, -um (adj.) – Hereditary

Herediarius, -ii (m.) – Heir

Heredito (1) – To Grant in Inheritance

Heres, Heredis – Heir, Heiress

Hic, Hec, Hoc (pronoun) – This, Those

153

Hinc – Hence

Hinc Inde – Hereupon

Homo, Hominis (m.) – Man

Honestus, -a, um (adj.) – Honest

Honor, -oris (m.) – Honour

Hospitium, -ii (n.) – Hospice, Hospital

Iaceo, -ere, Iacui, Iacitum (2) – To Lie (situate)

Ibdem – At, or In the same place

Idem (pronoun) – The same

Ille, Illa, Illud (pronoun) – That, Those

Imperpetuum (adv.) – In perpetuity

In – In, Into, On, At

Indicto (1) – To Indite

Ingulgentia, -e (f.) – Indulgence

Indulgeo, -ere, -dulsi, -dultum (2) – To Grant Indulgence

Infra (adv.) – Below, Within

Ingressus, -us (m.) – Entry

Inhibeo (2) – To Prevent

Iniuste (adv.) – Unjustly

Ad Instanciam – At the request

Insulta, -e (f.) – Assault

Insuper (adv.) – Above, As Mentioned

Inter (adv.) – Between

Intra (adv.) – Within

Intro (1) – To Enter

Intus (adv.) – Within

Ipse, Ipsa, Ipsum (pronoun) – Self

Is, Ea, Id (pronoun) – He, She, It, This, That

Iste, Ista, Istud (pronoun) – This

Ita (adv.) – So, Thus

Ius, Iuris (n.) - Law

Jacens, Jacentis (present participle) – lying

Jaceo, -ere, Jacui, Jacitum (2) – To Lie (situate)

Judeo, -ere, Jussi, Jussum (2) – To Order

Juramentum, -i (n.) – Oath

Juro (1) – To Swear

Juro Pro Fidelitate – To Swear Fealty

Jus, Juris (n.) - Law

De Jure – By Rights, By Claims

Largeo, -ere, -ui, -itum (2) – To Bestow

Largitas, -itatis (f.) – Width

Largus, -a, -um (adj.) – Wide

Latro, -onis (m.) – A Thief

Latus, -a, -um (adj.) – Wide

Lego (1) – To Bequeath

Lego, -ere, Legi, Lectum (3) – To Read

Leprosus, -i (m.) - Leper

Levo (1) – To Raise

Libellus, -i (m.) – Written Accusation

Liber, Libera, Liberum (adj.) – Free

Libra, -e (f.) – Pound (Money)

Loco (1) – To Lease, To Hire

Locus, -i (m.) – A Place

Longus, -a, -um (adj.) – Long

Magister, Magistri (m.) – Master

Magnus, -a, -um (adj.) – Great

Maior, Maius (adj.) – Greater

Male (adj.) – Badly

Malus, -a, -um (adj.) – Bad

Maneo, -ere, Mansi, Mansum (2) – To Dwell

Manerium, -ii (n.) – Manor

Mansum, -i (n.) – Dwelling-house

Marca, -e (f.) – A Mark (money)

Mater, Matris (f.) – Mother

Maximus, -a, -um (adj.) – Greatest

Melior, Melius (adj.) – Better

Mensis, -is (m.) – Month

Mercator, -oris (m.) – Merchant

Marcatum, -i (n.) – Market

Messuagium, -ii (n.) – A Messuage

Miles, Militis (m.) – Knight

Minister, -tri (m.) – Minor Official, Bailiff

Minor, Minus (adj.) – Lesser, Smaller

Missa, -i (f.) – Mass

Modo (adv.) – Only, Lately

Monacha, -e (f.) – Nun

Monachus, -i (m.) – Monk

Moneo (2) – To Warn

Moneta, -e (f.) – Coinage, Money

Moris, Mortis (f.) – Death

Terra Navita – Land held by villein tenure

Nativus, -i (m.) – Villein, Serf

Naturalis, -e (adj.) – Natural

Nec – Nor

Nomen, Nominis (n.) – Name

Non (adv.) – Not

Nos, Nostrum (pronoun) – We

Noster, -tra, -trum (adj.) – Our

Nunc (adv.) – Now, Present

Nuper (adv.) – Lately

Obedio, -ire, -ii or -ivi, -itum (4) – To Obey

Obeo (4) – To Die

Obitus, -us (m.) – Death

Obolus, -i (m.) – Half-Penny

Obsequium, -ii (n.) – Divine Service

Occupo (1) – To Occupy, Seize

Omnino (adv.) – Entirely

Omnis, -e (adj.) – All, Whole

Optime (adj.) – Best

Optimus, -a, -um (adj.) – Best

Orientalis, -e (adj.) – Eastern

Dies Palmarum – Palm Sunday

Papa, -e (m.) – The Pope

Papalis, -e (adj.) – Papal

Parca, -e (f.) – Park

Parcella, -e (f.) – Portion

Parco (1) – To Enclose

Paries, -etis (m.) – Wall

Parochia, -e (f.) – Parish

Parochialis, -e (adj.) – Parish

Pars, Partis (f.) – Part

Ex Parte – On behalf of

Per Partem – By means of

Pascha, -e (f.) – Easter Sunday

Proditio, -ionis (f.) – Treason

Sequela, -e (f.) – Issue

Sepelio (4) – To Bury

Guerra, -e (f.) – War

Secta, -e (f.) – Family

Printed in Great Britain
by Amazon